NEW DIRECTIONS FOR COMMUNITY COLLEGES

Arthur M. Cohen
EDITOR-IN-CHIEF

Florence B. Brawer
ASSOCIATE EDITOR

Changing Managerial Imperatives

Richard L. Alfred
University of Michigan

Patricia Carter
Community College Consortium

EDITORS

Number 84, Winter 1993

JOSSEY-BASS PUBLISHERS
San Francisco

ERIC®

Clearinghouse for Community Colleges

CHANGING MANAGERIAL IMPERATIVES
Richard L. Alfred, Patricia Carter (eds.)
New Directions for Community Colleges, no. 84
Volume XXI, number 4
Arthur M. Cohen, Editor-in-Chief
Florence B. Brawer, Associate Editor

Microfilm copies of issues and articles are available in 16mm and 35mm, as well as microfiche in 105mm, through University Microfilms Inc., 300 North Zeeb Road, Ann Arbor, Michigan 48106-1346.

LC 85-644753   ISSN 0194-3081   ISBN 1-55542-719-7

NEW DIRECTIONS FOR COMMUNITY COLLEGES is part of The Jossey-Bass Higher and Adult Education Series and is published quarterly by Jossey-Bass Inc., Publishers, 350 Sansome Street, San Francisco, California 94104-1342 (publication number USPS 121-710) in association with the ERIC Clearinghouse for Community Colleges. Second-class postage paid at San Francisco, California, and at additional mailing offices. POST-MASTER: Send address changes to New Directions for Community Colleges, Jossey-Bass Inc., Publishers, 350 Sansome Street, San Francisco, California 94104-1342.

SUBSCRIPTIONS for 1993 cost $49.00 for individuals and $72.00 for institutions, agencies, and libraries.

THE MATERIAL in this publication is based on work sponsored wholly or in part by the Office of Educational Research and Improvement, U.S. Department of Education, under contract number RI-93-00-2003. Its contents do not necessarily reflect the views of the Department or any other agency of the U.S. Government.

EDITORIAL CORRESPONDENCE should be sent to the Editor-in-Chief, Arthur M. Cohen, at the ERIC Clearinghouse for Community Colleges, University of California, 3051 Moore Hall, 405 Hilgard Avenue, Los Angeles, California 90024-1521.   May 5, 1994

Cover photograph © by Rene Sheret, After Image, Los Angeles, California, 1990.

Manufactured in the United States of America. Nearly all Jossey-Bass books, jackets, and periodicals are printed on recycled paper that contains at least 50 percent recycled waste, including 10 percent postconsumer waste. Many of our materials are also printed with vegetable-based inks; during the printing process, these inks emit fewer volatile organic compounds (VOCs) than petroleum-based inks. VOCs contribute to the formation of smog.

CONTENTS

EDITORS' NOTES

In an article published in 1986 entitled "Social Change and Community College Faculty," Richard L. Alfred described the effects of noninvolvement and called for reforms in governance to include new decision-making roles for faculty and staff. When that article was published, community colleges were growing at a pace that would move them from "supporting actors" to "stars" in the higher education world. The way colleges were organized or how they were managed was not an issue. Growth was the accepted barometer of success; as long as our colleges continued to grow, everything would be all right.

Almost a decade later, governance and management have become critical issues in public- and private-sector organizations. Industry giants such as General Motors, IBM, and Xerox are downsizing rapidly and changing the structure of their organizations to encourage worker involvement. Business leaders and organizational analysts have all but announced that teamwork is not just the current management fad—it is the new management. Max Weber's hundred-year-old multilayered bureaucratic pyramid is now being deconstructed to make way for flat organizations made up entirely of teams: faculty and staff teams, middle management teams, and executive teams. The old form of top-down decision making in an organization with many boundaries is slowly being replaced by the ideal of the "boundaryless organization"—one with minimal bureaucracy, where faculty and staff are open to ideas, have access to information, and are committed to serving customers. In view of this development and the increased importance of management structure and processes, the objectives of this volume are to examine key changes occurring in community college management and to identify future imperatives if our colleges are to maintain their competitive position.

The title of this volume is *Changing Managerial Imperatives*. In our view, it is inconceivable that fast-responding institutions such as community colleges can, or should, remain untransformed. One way or another, our colleges will adopt new approaches to management. Part One of the volume details the changing context for management. The opening chapter by Richard L. Alfred and Patricia Carter provides an overview of the changing management landscape and describes characteristics of institutions using old and new forms of management. Alfred and Carter question the extent to which community colleges are using myths from an earlier generation to guide management, and they identify important shifts needed to bring colleges into the customer-focused 1990s.

The next two chapters provide illustrations of new structures and approaches to management that have been implemented in colleges. In Chapter Two, Robert E. Parilla, a college president, describes his experience in transforming an institution with a bureaucratic management structure into a flat organization. Garth Jackson and Nancy Moulton, in Chapter Three, reveal another dimension to the transformation process, illuminating the importance of faculty and staff involvement in their Associates Model for Governance at Canadore College.

Following this introduction, the book shifts in Part Two to a vivid and practical description of management roles and responsibilities that faculty and staff will assume in transformed institutions. In Chapter Four, Albert L. Lorenzo emphasizes the importance of reality-based planning in a period of rapid change and tight resources. He provides insight into the pitfalls of planning models that do not consider the values and needs of internal and external customers while emphasizing process over product. Lorenzo's Strategic Guidance Model for planning is customer focused and user-friendly; but, most of all, it is a model that can be used by staff in every area of a college to make the frequent midcourse corrections that come with a customer service orientation.

Robbie Lee Needham's discussion of quality-focused management (QFM) in Chapter Five demonstrates the utility of QFM for faculty, staff, and administrators. Colleges interested in improving quality and customer service will have no choice but to turn to self-directed teams engaged in continuous process improvement, although that approach is a departure from established management practices.

James L. Hudgins, Sandi Oliver, and Starnell K. Williams close this section with a discussion of the importance of customer-oriented services, using Midlands Technical College's institutional effectiveness program as an example. They describe in detail the steps taken by the college to build a culture for student success through assessment and support services.

In Part Three, beginning with Chapter Seven, we take a look at some of the most critical issues facing leaders engaged in management transformation. Four issues interested us—creating personal networks, demonstrating integrity, leveraging diversity, and total quality orientation—and we selected two. Recognizing that many new faces in leadership will appear in the future, Ruth Burgos-Sasscer offers an illuminating look at the barriers that will need to be overcome in managing diversity. She describes the important characteristics of different groups that affect their outlook and approach to management and steps that leaders must take to create a climate of diversity. In Chapter Eight, Margaret Gratton provides an insightful look into features of the learning organization that will become every manager's domain in the future. Through anecdotes and examples, she delineates a context for leadership without elaborate structures, chain of command, and approving and authorizing. Personal networks are very important in this "boundaryless organization." Everyone is a leader because the ability to make things happen is learned within each part of the organization. David Deckelbaum concludes the volume in Chapter Nine with an annotated bibliography of sources and information on how changing community college management affects administrative roles and responsibilities.

Community colleges are at the center of the organizational changes sweeping communities and society. They do not need to be reinvented because they were designed and built only a few years ago as fast-changing, customer-focused institutions. Our invention is alive and well, but it is not organized and managed as well as it could be. We hope that this collection of articles will help practitioners become more aware of the transformation that must take place in the management of our colleges.

Richard L. Alfred
Patricia Carter
Editors

RICHARD L. ALFRED is associate professor of higher education at the University of Michigan and is author of more than seventy books, monographs, and articles on community college management, governance, and effectiveness.

PATRICIA CARTER is managing director of the Community College Consortium and is currently working on a national study of planning and strategic management practices in community colleges and the development of statewide effectiveness models.

PART ONE

Changing Context
for Management

Traditional management approaches may not serve colleges well in a market characterized by quality-conscious customers, aggressive competitors, and tightening resources.

Rethinking the Business of Management

Richard L. Alfred, Patricia Carter

General Motors versus Toyota, IBM versus Compaq, ABC versus CNN, Magnavox versus Sharp—by now the stories are well known of industry giants with strong reputations, deep pockets, and big market shares being displaced by competitors with far fewer resources but lean management and soaring expectations.

Interest in new approaches to management is bubbling up all over the community college landscape. The themes that reach across many of the current experiments are similar to management innovations in for-profit organizations: pushing decision-making responsibility down in the organization, involving faculty and staff in governance, and encouraging more active staff involvement in strategic tasks such as planning and assessment. The goal is to restructure management by involving more staff in big decisions that affect front-line services instead of bouncing decisions up the management ladder or issuing edicts from above.

What is surprising is that these changes are taking root in an institution that does not seem a likely candidate for innovation. Experiencing the momentum from swelling enrollments, educating half of all students entering the nation's colleges and universities over the last several years, community colleges have become large and potentially complacent organizations. The tradition of growth has been so consistent across our institutions that one can accurately predict the institutional success measures that will surface in conversations with administrators and survey research carried out with staff (Alfred and Linder, 1990; Alfred, Peterson, and White, 1992).

Administrators in other sectors of higher education often look at community colleges with envy and disdain. In addition to a legacy of substantial enrollment gains, community colleges appear to have many desirable characteristics: low cost, convenient access, a customer-oriented focus, programs and courses with seemingly important content that are easily filled, quick returns on education in the labor market, a comprehensive mission, multiple sources of funding, and a natural, supportive external constituency. Also, because of their instrumental approach to education, our colleges are largely untroubled by issues of political correctness, student activism, and debates about relevancy or the relationship of education to work.

"Confident" and "Eager" Community Colleges

Despite community colleges' apparent advantages, the forces for change in institutional management have gained strength in the 1990s. A growing number of stakeholders are coming to realize that traditional approaches to management may not work in a market characterized by quality-conscious customers, aggressive competitors, and tightening resources. Concerns are increasing about inconsistent program and service quality, slowed response to program markets, lack of innovative services, inadequate staff development, and inefficient resource allocation. What is striking about these concerns is that they are all basically management-induced and management-directed. Yet, despite concerns about their institutions' effectiveness, leaders are often at a loss as to how to go about making the necessary changes.

Administrators generally acquire their philosophy and style of management from graduate and professional education, peers and consultants, and, above all, their own career experiences. Over the years, repeated exposure to the risk-aversive, bureaucratic work environments that flourished in years of easy growth has produced a generation of administrators accustomed to making decisions and directing people. While this approach may be enough to maintain the institution's position, it cannot elicit the kind of energy and enthusiastic participation found in organizations that involve staff in the task of strategic management.

This may sound critical, but we believe it is possible to walk into almost any college and, through careful observation, quickly read the management climate. How are decisions made? What is it like to work there? How do faculty and staff approach problems? How cooperatively do they work? What is the pace? How do staff feel about their jobs? How committed are they to the institution?

To understand the effects of management climate on staff outlook and performance, imagine two community colleges in the same state competing in identical markets. "Confident" Community College, the recognized market leader, has accumulated a wealth of resources of every kind: talented faculty, state-of-the-art facilities and equipment, multiple sources of revenue, and industry support. It has been able to fund just about any initiative it has considered strategic. Over the years Confident adopted, and has successfully used, a top-down approach to management. But growth has obscured the underlying disease of underinvolvement. Nobody has noticed that the college is falling behind. The aspirations of faculty and staff to remain at the top of the market are assumed but in fact are declining. "How much do you need to worry," staff ask themselves, "when you are large, continue to grow, and have an enormous advantage over competitors?"

"Eager" Community College, a rival, is a relative latecomer to some of Confident's program markets. It is much smaller than Confident and has no choice but to make do with fewer people, a smaller budget, more modest facilities, and a fraction of Confident's discretionary resources. But Eager has every intention of competing successfully with Confident. To realize this ambition, it has decentralized the decision-making responsibility, empowering faculty and staff to search for undefined niches, develop innovative approaches to instruction and service delivery, and constantly assess customer needs and satisfaction, all while expending fewer resources than Confident. The misfit between Eager's resources and its aspirations would lead most observers to challenge the feasibility of its goals, if not the wisdom of its leaders.

But consider the likely effects of Confident's and Eager's approaches to management on how the two colleges frame their competitive strategies and use their human resources.

Clearly, Confident is much better placed to behave "strategically"—that is, to preempt Eager in attracting new student and employer markets, spend more on marketing and recruiting, develop new courses, purchase new technology, and so on. Confident's administrators are likely to continue their top-down approach to management, figuring that they can always outspend their smaller rival to get what they want. Faculty are likely to rest easily as long as growth continues at a rate sufficient to fill their classes and provide for their resource needs. They are also likely to disengage from the institution in favor of supplementary employment opportunities that provide two important advantages: additional income and the opportunity to personally control the work environment and compensate for the missing sense of true involvement at the college.

Eager, on the other hand, is likely to focus its resources on the soft side of the organization. This approach means involving faculty and staff in initiatives that improve quality and reduce costs: finding core competencies, assessing customer needs and satisfaction, building programmatic strategic plans, scanning external markets, identifying possibilities for collaboration with business, industry, and K–12 schools, and so on. Eager's administrators will strive to create a work environment that stresses speed, innovation, and a customer focus.

This outcome will not result from simply telling faculty and staff to be more innovative or directing them to be more quality-conscious. Eager's administrators will *institutionalize* a totally new approach to management, one in which standards are high, innovation is prized, staff are committed, and the focus is the future. They will create an institutional climate in which all players are working for the same institution and toward the same goals.

The argument here is substantially more subtle than the often-made point that colleges with empowered staff are more productive. What distinguishes Eager from Confident is not Eager's approach to management but the greater gap that exists between Eager's resources and its aspirations (Hamel and Prahalad, 1993). In contrast, Confident's problem is not that it is committed to top-down management (there is no inherent value in decentralized management) but that it has insufficient stretch in its aspirations. Confident's administrators and staff will not think and behave as if they were in a decentralized customer-focused college. What troubles Confident is a scarcity of ambition, not its approach to management.

Complexity, Control, and Complacency

If any of the characteristics of Confident College ring true for community colleges, two important questions arise: How did our colleges get into this situation, and what must be done to get them out of it? After all, at one time all community colleges were Eager-type organizations. They made do with few people, small budgets, and modest facilities as they developed programs and services to serve new markets. Is it possible for our colleges to become the victims of their own success?

The answer is yes. In his article "Corporate Redemption and the Seven Deadly Sins," Andrell Pearson describes the essence of waste in previously successful organizations (Pearson, 1992). Waste can happen in two ways. The first is erosion. As community colleges grow larger and more complex, the tasks of managing and involving staff in decisions become more and more difficult. There is a gradual erosion of the shared sense of mission that made the college special. New people do not know the problems that had to be overcome in building the institution, and continuing staff become so busy with administering and teaching that they do not take the time necessary to reinforce institutional values. Gradually the college drifts away from its mission and core values.

Complacency, the second source of waste, is a result of a number of easy-to-understand human factors. Growth in recent years has been automatic, and faculty and staff have learned that a certain level of effort will produce a certain level of results. Innovation has been reduced to what is essential and necessary within budget to produce acceptable change. Top administrators have devoted more and more attention to shaping public opinion by putting the most favorable spin on the college's performance. The result is a college success story for external consumption that may not accurately reflect internal staff perceptions of college performance. But over time, administrators come to accept cosmetic indicators of performance (for example, growth, visibility, and public recognition) as the truth.

Front-line faculty and staff are the first to recognize problems with quality. They are the first to know whether a college is overstaffed, bureaucratic, and slow to innovate and whether programs have lost touch with markets. But faculty and staff cannot talk directly with the board of trustees or external authorities, so they take their clues from top administrators. "If administration is satisfied, that is enough for me" becomes the prevailing attitude. Over time, the entire college compromises, rationalizes, relaxes, and settles down to a predictable work environment. Programs and services are organized to maintain harmony by operating at times and in locations convenient for staff. Faculty and staff become their own customers and begin to use the organization as an instrument for satisfying personal needs (Alfred, Peterson, and White, 1992).

To head off or escape the effects of this work environment, administrators need to confront myths in management that lead to complacency. Very simply, administrators must get the whole institution refocused on what is important in today's environment.

Two things really make a difference: avoiding incrementalism—the pervasive sentiment in established community colleges that this year's goal is to do what has been done before, only better—and encouraging staff actions that create value, such as improving instruction, delivering better services, developing collaborative ventures, and lowering costs.

Successful colleges realize that change is the new order and innovation is the primary driver. These colleges know that innovation is critical to their competitive success. They are constantly pushing resources and quality expectations down into the institution and taking care to translate them into terms that every academic department and service unit can understand.

Quality expectation and empowerment then become important tools for changing behavior. This attitude can be revealed through conversations with faculty and staff. In a national study of effective practices in community colleges, for example, Alfred and Linder (1990) found a remarkable consistency in the way faculty and staff described the operating philosophy: to be a multipurpose responsive organization, not just a postsecondary institution; to embrace paradox; to involve rather than exclude people. When staff use such dynamic words to describe the character of a college, administrators clearly have carefully considered the business of management in that college.

Are community colleges positioned for the future by virtue of their current approaches to management? Are they flexible, forward-looking organizations capable of adjusting to changes in the environment, or are they operating with management myths from a past in which the emphasis was on "managing people to manage growth"? The answer is yes and no. Community colleges are paradoxical organizations even in their approach to management. They employ multiple, sometimes contradictory, strategies for managing as a way of getting things done.

Challenging Myths of Management

Founding presidents of community colleges, the pioneers, had to be builders, political strategists, persuaders, organizers, master planners, and entrepreneurs. Their task was to bring order, to build and create, based on their own personal vision. Given their era and out of necessity, many brought with them traditional notions about management. Their performance, characterized by strong, results-oriented, powerful leadership, became the benchmark and formed the basis for management mythology in our colleges.

Management roles in today's community colleges evolved from traditional bureaucratic organizational structures that were hierarchical, top-down, and control-oriented. Bureaucracies were inherently autocratic. They were based on assumptions that vision was something developed at the top of the organization and that people would do exactly what they were told to do and not much else. Although it was helpful in organizing growing numbers of staff in a developing institution, this approach to management will not suit colleges in the quality-focused, customer-centered environment of the 1990s. Yet it continues to provide the underpinnings for our perception of what constitutes good management.

The question that needs to be asked if we are to organize our colleges, many of which look and act like Confident College, for a new wave of growth in customer service is this: Are bureaucratic management techniques ("myths") appropriate as colleges strive to achieve new goals in a climate of changed expectations? We believe that the answer is unequivocally no and that the sooner we can dispense with some of these myths, the sooner the transition back to Eager colleges can begin. Four myths, in particular, create the biggest barriers to change.

Security of Boundaries. In the corporate world, successful companies have eliminated nearly all distinctions between workers and managers. There are not people who do the thinking and people who do the work. All staff have input, and managerial and staff roles have been altered to produce "the boundaryless corporation"—a company without bureaucracy, in which people are curious, open, cooperative, and always breaking down barriers.

Confident College has many vestiges of the bureaucratic organization. Vision and strategy flow from the top; walls have been built that divide academic departments; support services and academic departments do not easily work together; and staff are not actively involved in institutionwide strategic activities (for example, planning and budgeting). Boundaries are a form of security, and their preservation is important. Why should nursing instructors work with automotive technology instructors to build a better general education curriculum? Why should counselors team up with librarians to develop better methods for delivering support services? Why should executive administrators work directly with faculty and staff in long-range institutional planning?

Tradition drives a lot of what we do. But, if programs and services do not meet the needs of customers, they have little value. Customer needs are constantly shifting and changing. To respond to these needs, faculty and staff need to make decisions quickly. Boundaried organizations with many management layers cannot make informed decisions quickly. Imagine going out in the cold with six sweaters on; your body does not know what the temperature is and is not quite sure how to react. A similar result occurs when information flows through many bureaucratic walls.

Leaders in Eager-type colleges working with limited resources have no choice but to get input from faculty and staff who know the work best. They cannot afford to support a dead or dying program. The more involved instructors and staff are in decisions, the more they own them, the better the decisions are, and, eventually, the faster they are made. Staff come to work feeling better about their jobs, and their aspirations become a resource working for the college rather than against it.

If It Isn't Broken, Why Fix It? To the leaders of Confident College, yesterday's successes make it tempting to ignore the need for change, yet the willingness to constantly acknowledge this need is the very essence of revitalization. The alternative is more of the same—a form of complacency in which colleges slowly but consistently lose ground.

To reverse our socialization and view criticism and critique as positive is difficult. All too often, acknowledging the need for change is interpreted as implying that institutions have been doing something wrong in the past. And it is natural to resist change. But leaders of Eager-type institutions encourage their followers to move past this cultural aversion. They take actions that help their institution to become self-regarding in ways that provide meaningful clues as to what will be needed to get to the top and stay on top. Eager institutions know that innovation is critical to their success. They are constantly in motion, doing things to make sure that there are enough innovations capable of changing the institution's future. Innovation is so critical to these colleges that they will reallocate resources, change staff, and alter management to make sure that innovation is going on in different places.

What really matters are big differences in program and service performance. A key to these big differences is reexamination of traditional assumptions about institutional structure and management. Reexamination, in turn, is driven by administrators and staff with small ideas that produce management breakthroughs. Small ideas crop up everywhere in the college, not just at the top. Management's role is to move ideas quickly so they can be examined, decided on, and implemented. This is the essence of innovation. Innovative colleges are willing to take a hard, critical look at their structure, systems, and procedures from a very different perspective. They free innovation and initiative from the walls of bureaucracy by moving beyond questions about consistency and control to questions such as these: "How does this affect the customer?" "Do we really need this?" "How does it support the efforts of people to improve this college?" They critique their assumptions regularly in an effort to truly incorporate continuous improvement notions into their ways of doing business on a day-to-day basis.

Revitalized colleges do not simply ask, "Is it broken?" They ask, "Is it the best it can be?" However, openness to critique and willingness to innovate require abandoning other myths related to institutional leadership.

Leadership Equals Rank, Power, and Control. The positional power of the early college leaders was very important. It worked; authority at the top was seldom challenged. Faculty and staff expectations did not include being involved in "big picture" decision making. A great deal needed to be done very quickly, and ambiguity (some called it "flexibility") was necessary as community colleges attempted to establish their place in the postsecondary community. Someone, or some group, needed to call the shots, define boundaries, establish a framework. Leaders were looked to for strength and clarification during these formative stages.

As leaders shifted their emphasis from structure to strategies to cope with rapid growth and respond to contemporary challenges of planning, assessment, and institutional effectiveness, the need to involve others in a wider range of initiatives became clear. Presidents, deans, and other leaders began to recognize that in order to foster involvement, power had to be shared and that the institution's ultimate strength would come from the synergistic efforts of its stakeholders. There is only one way to break down the walls of bureaucracy and share power, and that is for the president to drive it personally. This task usually requires refocusing the president's job. It is not enough to pledge to change. The president must shed many administrative duties to spend more time on encouraging staff initiative and involvement.

At too many of our colleges, we still see cases of "executive treadmill." Afflicted presidents spend much of their time in ceremonial activities, staff meetings, dog and pony shows, community relations activities, and pro forma institutional performance reviews. They end up getting most of their information through simplified staff analyses that have little to do with better results and much to do with insisting on uniformity and second-guessing throughout the institution. In effect, these presidents have become the "chief administrative officer" instead of the "chief quality officer"—the driving force for team management to improve quality and achieve important institutional goals. As a consequence, if you ask faculty and staff, "How much does the president know about your program or service?" the answer usually is, "Very little except for signing off on budget or major decisions."

In the past, good leaders by virtue of their rank were expected to know the right answers. In today's community colleges, good leaders must know how to ask the right questions. Rather than being omnipotent experts, leaders of revitalized colleges tap the total human resource potential of their institutions. As opposed to telling, they use questions to encourage, prompt, and guide. They listen, and they encourage staff to question every practice instead of accepting the status quo. They give staff much latitude in how to do things, and they install systems to be sure people are working together to solve problems. They encourage staff involvement and delegate decision making, but they make sure that leaders throughout the institution understand the changing educational market, the college's competitive position, and what needs to be done to improve performance. They have a mind-set that aims to help staff succeed, not give them orders and catch their mistakes.

Leadership Means Promoting a Personal Vision. The personal vision of the leader, certainly critical in the early years as our colleges established their place in postsecondary education, provided strength and reassurance for followers. But the "trust me" days are gone. Personal vision is being replaced by the need for a shared vision. And the invitation to participate in the college's definition is being extended beyond the campus to involve stakeholders in the community as well. What college can afford to neglect the opinion of employers and other interest groups in decisions about educational programs? Our colleges are being asked to establish linkages and collaborations with a variety of partners; this extended form of operation is apt to become more important in the future.

Presidents and deans are beginning to get directly involved with key customers and staff working on major problems, and they get feedback from several sources, not just direct reports. They are beginning to spend their time differently at work, mostly by interacting with staff in small groups or individually, not sitting in formal meetings or reading staff reports. They move to where the action is instead of trying to replicate it in the office. Through the use of focus groups, community surveys, and customer satisfaction measures, leaders are listening to, acknowledging, and recognizing the messages coming from within and without and making use of this "intelligence" to fashion a vision that is consistent with the institution's value base and its constituents' aspirations. They know that it is commitment, rather than mere compliance, that will make it possible to stretch the college's aspirations, and they are willing to take the time to be certain that a vision is in place that will evoke commitment. They know that good leaders do not push—they pull.

Many other myths prevail, of course. But eliminating just these four from our thinking about what constitutes good management is a major step toward removing critical obstacles to the work that needs to be done.

Imperatives for Tomorrow

Having made the point that we believe it is important for colleges to rethink the way in which they approach management, we acknowledge that the process is neither quick nor easy. The challenge of getting from A to B, or from Confident to Eager, will take time and patience, intuition and knowledge, and consistency of word with action.

Traditionally, creating change in our colleges has not been difficult. Management reorganizations involving a change of players are common. Every college has tried a new institutional improvement program or process, such as management by objectives, quality circles, or other imported strategies. More recently, our colleges have been looking at total quality management and continuous quality improvement programs as ways to do better with less.

Whatever the strategy, we must remember that these "fixes" do not work in and of themselves. Two critical elements need to be thoroughly explored by the college before embarking on any change strategy: cultural fit and cultural preparation. Cultural fit relates to the strategy's appropriateness to the institution, its fit with important characteristics. Prior to implementation, the college must address questions such as these: What is our history? What is our reality? What are we really like? What is our ideal? What would we like to be if we could? How big is the gap between reality and the ideal? What is our comfort level with the changes we will have to make?

Cultural preparation refers to resources—staff, money, talent, experience, and so forth—a college has available to implement a management change. To determine cultural preparation, other questions need to be asked: What skills are needed and available? What do we have to learn to do, or learn to do better? What are the structural barriers that will impede our reaching the ideal?

The temptation to delegate these questions to a task force or small working group must be avoided; dialogue must be opened to the entire college community. This approach will most likely require a rethinking of the college's current notions about the meaning and the roles of management.

From Management to Leadership. While traditionally managers were expected to control and direct, leaders in innovative colleges today are redirecting their energy toward creating healthy cultures and managing the necessary evolution that will allow the college and its stakeholders to prepare for adaptation. These leaders use noncoercive strategies that are more concerned with orchestrating and coordinating than controlling. They are what Bennis calls "social architects" (1976, p. 169). Rather than relying on authority and command, these college leaders use their political skills to identify issues, persuade, build coalitions, campaign for points of view, and serve constituencies.

Examples of collaboration within colleges are appearing more and more frequently: mutual gains bargaining, full participation of collective bargaining representatives on senior-level college decision-making bodies, concerns about routinely assessing morale, and explicitly acknowledging that faculty and staff are important "internal customers." Kanter (1989) describes this as being able to operate without the safety net of hierarchical power. It involves redirecting the college's effort toward building respect for authority through relationship building, shifting the focus from competition to a common concern for excellence, and consistently operating with the highest ethical standards.

This shift in emphasis will likely be more difficult for some managers to accept than others, but inherent in it is a rethinking of where good leaders best spend their time and where their attention is most usefully directed.

From Control to Outcome Accountability. Abandoning micromanagement is a key step in fostering innovation in community colleges. Strategies that reflect the leadership paradigm of consolidated power and top-down control are being replaced with a whole new set of priorities and ways of measuring outcomes.

Implied in this broad-brush statement are several important qualifiers. In order to focus on accountability, all players need to have a full understanding of both the priorities and the expectations of the institution. Administrators who are uncomfortable with unleashing power within an institution often counter that "you simply cannot have everyone running off and taking initiatives at will," which, of course, is very true. However, if the college has a well-articulated strategic plan in place and individuals' roles, resources, and limitations related to the plan have been translated and communicated effectively, the need for step-by-step monitoring and reporting is eliminated. In an innovative college, stakeholders feel free to act, within realistic limits, and contribute, in a meaningful way, to achieving the college's goals. If staff believe that their contributions are meaningful, they are more likely to stay involved and encourage others to do so.

From Complacency to Involvement. Active participation in decision making, in some form, is an objective in most community colleges. A host of committees, councils, task forces, and decision-making groups can be found. Yet a common concern raised by administrators is the difficulty in finding faculty and staff who are willing to become involved.

In most colleges the same core group of committed individuals regularly volunteer to assist with new initiatives while the majority remain on the sidelines or on the fence. Tapping this underutilized resource could provide the college with a rich source of new ideas and energy. The trick becomes how one goes about doing it. Identifying the source of the apathy is an important first step as it provides necessary clues about its reversal. Past experiences may have led certain individuals to feel that expending the extra effort to become involved is not worth it. Too often our structures provide for "psychological participation"—participation that leaves the impression of truly being involved—when in fact the decisions being made are relatively inconsequential.

For instance, unless the process is clearly articulated, faculty may be involved in identifying and ranking capital priorities for their department, but actual decisions about how the funds will be allocated are made at the chairperson's or dean's level. The misunderstandings and disappointments that ensue discourage future involvement. Or, as one faculty member put it, "They ask us what we think, and we tell them. But they go ahead and do what they were going to do anyway. It's like talking into a black hole. And sooner or later you just stop talking."

Achieving involvement requires interest and substantive participation in the institution's decision making. It demands active involvement in decision making about significant issues. It implies that the involvement of the stakeholders in determining the direction of the institution, in getting involved in the "bigger picture," crosses functional and hierarchical boundaries. It acknowledges that a variety of perspectives can enrich the ultimate decision and that regardless of rank or title, the more skills that can be brought together around the table, the better off the college will be.

To achieve such involvement, it is important to rethink the way in which information is shared within the college. This shift means reexamining traditional notions about what is "confidential" and committing to the open sharing of facts and figures that may, at times, not be complimentary but nevertheless truly reflect current reality. It requires an investment of time and resources to ensure that all staff using information have an understanding of the issues to which the information is addressed. All too often, participation breaks down when those involved do not have the same knowledge base or understanding of the task requirements.

A good example of a breakdown caused by lack of knowledge is the practice of "rapid immersion strategic planning" used by some colleges. Executive administrators form strategic planning task forces by inviting representatives from a diagonal slice of the organization to ensure adequate representation from the various constituencies. The task force jumps in and gets going on the task of planning without taking the time to be sure that its members share a common understanding of what constitutes good planning, without coming to agreement on a common set of planning definitions, and without clarifying collective objectives. Ultimately, frustrations surface that undermine individual members' sense of pride and ownership in the process and the product. These unsatisfying experiences make it unlikely that the individual will be willing to volunteer again or that planning will produce important results.

Taking care to ensure that the training and resource needs of the players are addressed is an important step in encouraging and in reducing the distance that all too often exists between the academic and administrative cultures within our colleges.

From Isolation to Integration. Some argue that cultural dualism—the separation of the academic or faculty culture from the administrative or "corporate" culture—is an inevitable barrier to college-wide involvement. While it is important to acknowledge the differences in priorities and even, in some cases, definitions used by "academics" as opposed to "administrators," ways to create bridging experiences that will inform and integrate rather than perpetuate isolation need to be sought.

Integration involves helping each group gain experience with and information about the issues and problems facing the other. It entails encouraging staff to find out what is going on in other departments and service units, even if the relationship is unclear or unimportant. Integrated colleges foster respect for the expertise of different groups; they acknowledge the reality that each has its own priorities within its own domain and that each is entitled to have a greater voice in certain kinds of decisions. But the focus is on a common set of goals and values that emphasize solidarity rather than differences.

Leaders in integrated colleges know that an important part of their function is to help constituents "connect the dots"—to explain the linkages and the importance of the institution's strategic initiatives. They foster a sense of "us" as opposed to the traditional "we/they" dichotomy. It is easy to forget that the importance of a new college initiative may not be self-evident to all of its members. In the absence of clearly communicated connections, faculty and staff often view new priorities as merely this year's management fad. The interconnections need to be explained, the objectives clearly linked to important improvements, and relevance made explicit.

Conclusion

What have tended to be management-induced and management-directed concerns in community colleges about improving quality, enhancing ability to respond to program markets, innovation and responsiveness, and staff development during times of resource constraint need to become the shared concerns and issues of the broader college community. We suggest that this shift can only happen if we are willing to reopen the dialogue about how we can best approach the management of our institutions.

Reexamining the status quo, dispensing with myths that impede our ability to be creative and innovative, and making changes where necessary to restructure management by involving more staff in decisions that affect frontline services are important first steps. "Eager," revitalized colleges—those that will thrive, not simply survive—will be those that emphasize leadership over management, accountability over control, involvement over complacency, and integration over isolation.

Certainly there are no quick fixes, but a sufficient number of success stories in community colleges today prove that it can be done. The question is, Are leaders willing to spend the time and energy rethinking the business of management?

References

Alfred, R. L., and Linder, V. P. Rhetoric to Reality: Effectiveness in Community Colleges. Ann Arbor, Mich.: Community College Consortium, 1990.

Alfred, R. L., Peterson, R. O. and White, T. H. Making Community Colleges More Effective: Leading Through Student Success. Ann Arbor, Mich.: Community College Consortium, 1992.

Bennis, W. The Unconscious Conspiracy. New York: AMACOM Books, 1976.

Hamel, G., and Prahalad, C. K. "Strategy as Stretch and Leverage." Harvard Business Review, Mar.–Apr. 1993, p. 77.

Kanter, R. M. When Giants Learn to Dance. New York: Simon & Schuster, 1989.

Pearson, A. E. "Corporate Redemption and the Seven Deadly Sins." Harvard Business Review, May–June 1992, p. 72.

RICHARD L. ALFRED is associate professor in the Higher and Adult Continuing Education Program at the University of Michigan, Ann Arbor, and founding director of the Community College Consortium.

PATRICIA CARTER is managing director of the Community College Consortium, which is cosponsored by the University of Michigan and Michigan State University and operates out of the Center for the Study of Higher and Postsecondary Education at the University of Michigan, Ann Arbor.

An adaptive institution is one that knows a lot about itself through faculty and staff who are involved in identifying challenges and in creating programs to meet changing needs.

Adapting Institutional Structure and Culture to Change

Robert E. Parilla

Human beings revere and rejoice in the birth process; it symbolizes renewal and hope and often taps into, stirs, or enlivens our best impulses. A birth can inspire a deeply felt sense of optimism, well-being, and increased appreciation for life's possibilities. Any noble or mundane beginning reflects some of these positive feelings, whether it is the initial stages of a grand project or the first day of a new semester. So too with higher education; however lofty, each institution began as an idea that committed and talented people nurtured into reality.

Many community colleges were created in the high-energy, "boundless horizons" period after World War II. As the GI Bill sent thousands of veterans home with money and encouragement to invest in education and training, communities responded by setting up programs wherever there was space—in high schools, libraries, even garages. All that seemed necessary were a classroom, a course, and a teacher. Classes were welcomed and filled; both the challenge and response were very satisfactory to those involved. Faculty came from secondary classrooms and counseling offices, other colleges and business and industry with a common desire to teach. A student-centered rather than research-accented focus prevailed in the early assignment. It was an adventure. The early college communities had a pioneer spirit that encouraged teamwork, cooperation, and flexibility.

Founding administrators communicated the message that a concept was being mobilized. The participation of all players was both significant and necessary. Each college has its legendary story, such as the dean who became tired of faculty requests for phone lines and installed a pay phone or the facilities manager who received a hundred not quite adult-sized desks because the school supply company figured "junior college" must be a misprint of "junior high." Many faculty who are still teaching were part of those days and usually reminisce with a sense of loss, even though, of course, everyone now has a phone, the desks are the proper size, and the instructional environment is immensely improved and supported by all manner of high-technology wizardry.

Success Has Some Casualties

When the Higher Education Act of 1965 passed, there were 654 two-year colleges. By 1985 there were 1,350 two-year colleges, representing more than 40 percent of institutions of higher education and accounting for 44 percent of all first-time college freshmen (Adelman, 1991, p. 1). Individual enrollments soared. In the boom years of the 1960s community colleges were opening at the rate of one per week and growing rapidly to meet baby boomers' demands. By the 1980s these colleges were attempting to accommodate enrollment growth, state control, proliferating local demands, new student constituencies, and collective bargaining. The seemingly endless pool of students allowed many institutions to settle into the comfort of tradition, control, and complacency—a circumstance that affected the organizational development of many community colleges.

Procedures, set up to facilitate necessary functions when an institution is small, run the risk of evolving into rigid guidelines. Often a rule can endure long after the original reason for establishing a procedure is forgotten. As fledgling institutions with a desire for quality and standards of excellence, community colleges invented rules and procedures as they were needed. Over time a hierarchy for management developed and rules proliferated, giving community colleges many of the characteristics of a complex bureaucracy.

The community college concept, based on identifying and serving the postsecondary needs of a local area, can suffer from this kind of rule-driven, tight hierarchy. The board of trustees and senior administrators may derive a sense of legitimacy and safety from this controlled environment, but front-line administrators, faculty, and staff quietly protest since the ability to execute an idea is diminished and responsiveness is slowed to a sluggish pace. Individuals attempting to respond to perceived changes with innovative instructional approaches, creative programs, or different strategies can be frustrated by a system that has lost resilience and has replaced flexibility with form or a set of standard practices.

Such influences are not easy to pinpoint. The institution continues to grow and appears to be well-run and efficient. Students are content, and faculty seem satisfied with a system that makes all the necessary decisions but does not intrude into classrooms. Only when responsiveness to change or the issue of climate and morale comes into the spotlight (as in an opportunity for curriculum development or an institutional self-study for accreditation) do the frustrations and tension surface. Recognizing the dynamics at work and their larger implications for institutional development provides college leaders with an opportunity for renewal through self-analysis.

Structure and Function Mismatch

Many of today's large multicampus comprehensive community colleges were once small friendly enterprises. Early colleges were often adjuncts of the local secondary school system (Cohen and Brawer, 1989, p. 4). The rigid hierarchies that evolved to administer many community colleges are no doubt at least partly a legacy from the public school bureaucracy. As demands increased from local and state agencies for cost control and growth, centralized planning proliferated, and so did managerial hierarchies. The organizational structure most commonly used to manage growth in many colleges is the controlled pyramid of secondary education.

Involving centralized control and top-down decision making, the pyramidal organization does not fit the community college concept particularly well. Our colleges have been built on a tradition of innovation and efficiency in responding to local needs. Their goals are to provide for the learning needs and wants of the community (Cohen and Brawer, 1989, p. 7). To continue to modify and tailor instructional programs and services to local needs, a responsive and flexible management system is needed.

Many community colleges are beginning to discover a mismatch of form and function. There is a growing realization that some institutions have become entities whose structure may be impeding progress. These are institutions with high-quality instructional programs, highly qualified faculty, and well-run support units. However, they have become static, and the energy and creativity of the early days has largely disappeared.

The Adaptive Institution

The strength of any organization is founded in self-knowledge and a continuous process of analysis and renewal. Clarity of purpose invigorates the mission of an institution and encourages creativity and risk taking. An adaptive institution is one that knows a lot about itself through faculty and staff who are involved in identifying challenges and in creating programs to meet changing needs.

To fulfill their mission of service and timely response to local community needs, community colleges must anticipate changes in the environment, cope with changing educational needs, and be sensitive to fluctuating demographics and shifting political imperatives. A rigid hierarchical organization does not allow for the free flow of information and dialogue among units needed to adapt to change. Success is more likely in an organization whose culture acknowledges that everyone must, at least occasionally, be a leader.

We can use trends in the emerging economy to illustrate the importance of management structure in adapting to change. To be in the forefront of change, community colleges must anticipate and respond to the needs of an economy whose competitive edge is the skill level of its work force. Traditionally community colleges have provided access to education and training for students who have been excluded by the selective and linear nature of four-year postsecondary programs. Today the information age is here. Women will make up 64 percent of the new entrants to the work force by the year 2000 (Adelman, 1992, p. 1). The United States is experiencing the greatest wave of immigration in a hundred years (Garreau, 1992). The fastest-growing segment of the U.S. labor force will soon be minorities. The fastest-growing segment of society will consist of those who are living below the poverty level. To compete with the economy of a global village that offers limitless cheap labor and tax incentives, the United States must counter with the intelligence and skill of an educated and highly skilled work force.

The task before community college leaders is to shape institutions that will be comfortable with these new realities. Colleges must be prepared to adapt curricula and support services to the changing marketplace and to the changing study body, not only offering traditional transfer, technical, and developmental programs but also marketing responsive packages of training and skill development. Alternate delivery systems for instructional programs will grow in importance as the need to reach large audiences of students with shrinking or static resources increases.

A management model that values continuous improvement and is sensitive to external pressures must be nurtured if community colleges are to deal with the shifting demands of the global marketplace. This model is the core feature of an organization we know as the "adaptive community college"—a college in which decentralized decision making and personal empowerment along with shared vision of institutional purpose and accountability for results get things done. Decentralized control is a risky venture that must be balanced by the development of a common purpose and set of values. The challenge for leaders is to promote a common culture that is imbued with the principles of teamwork, flexibility, and continuous improvement. Perhaps the most critical element is the functioning of cross-unit, task-centered teams committed to student success.

Continuous Quality Improvement: A Resource, Not a Panacea

The concept of continuous quality improvement has gained increasing visibility as a strategy to solve a host of perceived concerns in modern organizations. A focus on continuous improvement can provide a useful framework for change if there is an organizational philosophy in place that is open to change and willing to adapt. Current definitions focus on six facets that can transform an organization (Tuttle, 1989, p. 4), all with relevance to community colleges in transition:

Make constant improvement the number one priority. Reframe the mission to focus on assisting more students to achieve their educational goals successfully.

Focus on students and co-workers as service receivers. Build students' perspectives into every aspect of the college, with faculty and staff thinking of themselves as part of internal service units where they are both the users and providers of services.

Focus on prevention. Program carefully for appropriate assessment, advising, and placement designed to increase a student's likelihood of success.

Manage by data. Rely on assessment to determine the progress and goal achievement of entering students, and use information for planning and revising programs.

Encourage total employee involvement. Foster an environment in which faculty and staff feel connected to the teaching/learning process, take ownership and accountability, and feel that the organization supports and appreciates their efforts.

Establish a cross-functional administration. Communicate freely without regard to the structure of the organization, with authority and decision making based on expertise as close to the need as possible.

The principles and underlying values of continuous quality improvement foster a workplace that allows people to grow, make use of their abilities, increase in self-esteem, and make a valued contribution. However, quality improvement principles should be viewed as a resource for change, not a panacea. Adopting continuous quality improvement from a formulaic approach will not work for community colleges. Administrators and faculty express a natural resistance to the bottom-line philosophy of business that equates customer satisfaction to increased profits. In addition, there are real differences in measuring outcomes according to product control rather than service satisfaction. Although the principles and techniques of a continuous quality improvement process apply equally well to services, business, and manufacturing, the difference between services and products creates problems when applying a product-oriented approach to a service-oriented organization.

The concept of continuous quality improvement can nonetheless be integrated into the culture of a community college. Each instructor and staff member who makes a commitment to an ongoing assessment of personal performance contributes personally to a climate of excellence. Individual accountability and a sense of shared responsibility for student success must take root as institutional values. The relationship of rising customer satisfaction to increasing profits validates the emphasis on excellence and service in the private sector. But the rewards for educators are more elusive. They are integrated into the gratification that each member of the college community experiences through vicarious successes of students. In community colleges we have always used materials at hand to promote learning and growth.

Continuous quality improvement can be a vehicle for organizational change if the goal is to improve teaching and learning, not to evaluate faculty or staff.

Are other options available to community college leaders as they attempt to adapt organizational structure to changing student and community needs? Do other remedies exist for community colleges experiencing a midlife crisis? Borrowing from the ideas of management pundits such as Peters and Waterman (1982) and the tenets of continuous quality management, but adapting them to the culture of community colleges, I suggest the following approach to organizational change:

Recognize the problem. Hierarchies, formal communication systems, and policies that encourage the status quo create a climate of lethargy in which student and community needs become problems to be addressed rather than opportunities for challenge or creative problem solving. Initiative and ownership are discouraged, and existing practices remain intact, which thereby deters innovation.

Prescribe remedies. It is essential to refocus the college mission on changing community educational needs rather than existing programs and practices. The following principles should be promoted:

Stress shared values: Institutional values such as the primacy of teaching and learning, personal empowerment, mutual trust, openness, and dedication to student development and excellence should be internalized by the college community.

Have a bias for action: The institution should encourage a work ethic in which individuals are willing to take on problems and act rather than look the other way.

Personalize the "customer" (student): The concept of meeting student needs should become the orientation of every college office.

Encourage autonomy and entrepreneurship: Every member of the college community should take ownership for individual professional contributions, become informed, and be ready to make changes as needed.

Foster productivity through people: Dynamic change should become an honored value that is anticipated rather than feared.

Keep the approach simple and staff lean: Bureaucratic procedures and administrative layers of review should be kept to a minimum.

Balance control and latitude: The development of judgment and decision-making skills should be encouraged at every level of the institution.

Equate organizational change with growth. Flattening the hierarchy and pushing authority toward the student and service user will stimulate the institution.

Build a shared vision around common values. Especially important are the following values: student needs first, community assessment and feedback, program assessment for quality and efficacy, free-flowing information, decision making involving those affected and at the most practical level, accountability

Table 2.1. Decision-Making Processes in Community Colleges

Processes	Hierarchical Model	Decentralized Model
Exercise of authority	Centralized	Delegated
Leadership and management	Controlling	Facilitating
Monitoring	External supervision (central data review)	Internal ownership (data gathering, reviewing, reporting)
Regulation	Prescriptive	Personal empowerment
Accountability	Process oriented	Results oriented
Planning	Long term, centralized	Unit based, opportunity oriented, ad hoc, long term
Outcomes	Minimum standard	Continuous improvement
Communication	Hierarchical	Ad hoc
External orientation (students, community)	Confrontation	Proactive
Internal orientation (Co-workers)	Competitive	Cooperative

for improved results accompanying decision making, self-actualization facilitated by supervisors, and student feedback driving innovation and improvement.

Certain operational functions are intrinsic in any organization; the critical difference is in how these are handled. By recasting their administrative processes, community colleges can change their organizational culture. For example, a major departure from traditional management is the movement from centralized to decentralized control. In the hierarchical organization characteristic of many of our colleges, information goes up, and a decision comes down. Decentralization distributes authority throughout the institution by delegating responsibility for decision-making. Table 2.1 reviews important differences in the approach to decision-making.

In a decentralized model, leadership facilitates change rather than controlling behavior. Accountability is based on results and responsiveness rather than following a series of procedures. Output is measured by continuous evaluation rather than minimum standards. Inculcating a new management vision comes slowly, but the process is an invigorating and empowering experience for a college community. Once faculty and staff begin to believe in their own creative potential for continuous improvement, the course is set. The organization will continue to develop; a revitalization of spirit and commitment will have taken root.

A Case Study in Revitalization

Montgomery College in Maryland may be seen as an example of the difficulty involved in moving a well-run, solid, and seasoned institution beyond "very good" to "outstanding." The college, founded in 1946, has grown from a small tightly knit academic community of fifteen faculty to a complex three-campus system with more than eleven hundred full-time employees. Over time, a structured hierarchy of administrators and supervisors evolved that controlled operations through highly formalized rules that governed every corner of operations and were compiled into an institutional bible known as the Policies and Procedures Manual. Communication was controlled by a strictly enforced protocol of signatures. Each campus was tightly administered by a provost, who reported to an academic vice president. This officer, along with a vice president for administrative services and a vice president for planning, made up a central administration that included directors of support functions and reported directly to the president.

As Montgomery College entered its fifth decade, the institution had grown to over 460 full-time faculty, 130 academic programs, 23,000 credit students, and 22,000 noncredit students managed through a bureaucratic structure as shown in Figure 2.1. Externally the college enjoyed a well-deserved reputation for quality. Nevertheless, response time to outside initiatives was slow. Internally the system had come to lack spontaneity and the mutually supportive culture that characterized the early days of the institution.

By 1987 stresses were becoming apparent. "Turf" issues among the campuses were becoming more acrimonious, and staff were increasingly isolated by narrowly interpreted parameters of responsibility and specialization. During 1985–86 the president had dozens of meetings with small groups (five to eight people) of employees to discuss the college and its potential. These meetings revealed that faculty and staff felt that Montgomery College was an institution of high quality, a place where they liked to work but felt stifled by policy, lack of recognition, and limited understanding of their work.

An accreditation self-study completed in 1987 confirmed this underlying sense of dissatisfaction and lowered morale. While these issues were not seen as threatening to the life of the institution, they were indicative of a general malaise that was keeping the college from achieving its potential. Urged by the board of trustees, the president began a six-month sabbatical to reflect on the present needs and future direction of the college.

After a great deal of reading, contemplation, and discussion, the president returned to the college and launched an initiative dubbed "revitalization." Revitalization (with philosophical roots in the writing of Tom Peters, John Kotter, John Gardner, and others, as well as the literature of total quality management) was specifically tailored to the unique circumstances of Montgomery College. It was designed to reaffirm the commitment of the college to teaching and learning within a work ethic of personal initiative and empowerment, individualized recognition, teamwork, risk taking, and high-quality performance.

The central goal, simply stated, was to revitalize a large complex college that by most standards was doing a good job but was plagued by problems of communication, bureaucracy, individual isolation, and too much structure. All

Figure 2.1. Montgomery College's Revised Organizational Chart

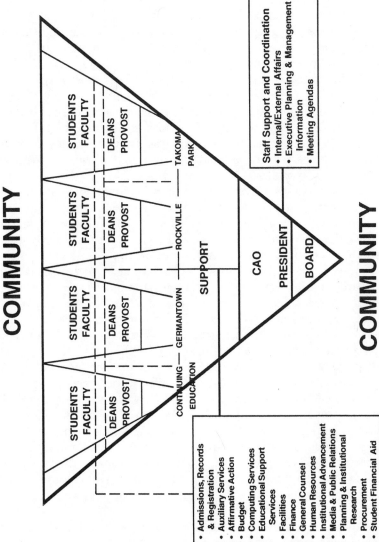

COMMUNITY

COMMUNITY

STUDENTS
FACULTY

STUDENTS
FACULTY

STUDENTS
FACULTY

STUDENTS
FACULTY

DEANS
PROVOST

DEANS
PROVOST

DEANS
PROVOST

DEANS
PROVOST

CONTINUING
EDUCATION

GERMANTOWN

ROCKVILLE

TAKOMA
PARK

SUPPORT

CAO

PRESIDENT

BOARD

Staff Support and Coordination
• Internal/External Affairs
• Executive Planning & Management
  Information
• Meeting Agendas

• Admissions, Records
  & Registration
• Auxiliary Services
• Affirmative Action
• Budget
• Computing Services
• Educational Support
  Services
• Facilities
• Finance
• General Counsel
• Human Resources
• Institutional Advancement
• Media & Public Relations
• Planning & Institutional
  Research
• Procurement
• Student Financial Aid

of these factors made it cumbersome for individuals to accomplish routine procedures, let alone to look for new opportunities to be innovative.

The first step was to flatten the organization. The vice-presidential level of
the hierarchy was eliminated, and a chief administrative officer (CAO) was
appointed to be a part of the office of the president. Bureaucratic barriers were
eliminated, and the whole college community was called on to participate in
an effort to reshape the institution through a personal commitment to continuous improvement. The major objective was to galvanize the college community and infuse the institution, once again, with some of the excitement,
creativity, teamwork, and shared purpose of serving the community's educational and training needs.

The first reaction of the college community was shock, as the organizational structure flattened out and the hierarchy crumbled. Communication was
opened up throughout the system and decision making pushed close to the
level of service, as shown in Figure 2.1. The administrative level closest to the
teaching and learning process, the deans, was given significantly more authority. They were charged with facilitating change and engaging the talents of faculty in a new approach to their responsibilities.

The sixteen deans represented the crucial communication link to 460 full-
time faculty and, through the faculty, to students and the community. Formerly
these deans had been insulated from the president by three administrative layers; now they met directly to surface and review issues. The provosts, previously the controlling administrators on campus, were asked to function as
facilitators, coaches, and mentors. The former role of the cabinet as a sound-
ing board on legal issues, public relations, and other topical concerns was
altered. The reconfigured cabinet, composed of the CAO, the provosts of the
campuses and continuing education, the chair of the faculty assembly, and the
chair of the staff senate now functioned as a team to consider the college's
major educational issues and articulate them to the rest of the institution.

Several issues rapidly emerged. The culture of control was deeply embed-
ded in the organization. The roles and the expectations were new, but the players were not. Many administrators bitterly regretted what they perceived as a
loss of control in the new culture of shared power. Others felt unprepared for
their new responsibilities. The human resources staff, for example, had an
exquisitely honed hierarchy of training opportunities for specific needs—
supervisory skills, professional development, and so on. They were not prepared to hear that they would play a critical role in building and nurturing a
new culture of continuous improvement, personal empowerment, and team
effort.

Although it was anticipated that the process of change would be slow and
incremental, resistance and misunderstanding among the administrative team
were surprising. The constituencies of the institution reacted to revitalization
in different ways. The board of trustees, for example, supported the idea. Some
administrators were excited and energized by the change; others were petri-

fied. Faculty were skeptical but enthusiastic about the concept. Staff members, baffled by hearing that they were to use initiative and personal judgment after years of rigid control by supervisors, were mostly confused. Students, major potential beneficiaries of revitalization, were oblivious.

Nurturing a New Culture. Providing a rationale for change was the most critical element in the early stages of revitalization. Montgomery College had become a comfortable, predictable environment—one in which most instructors and staff believed they were contributing to quality rather than impeding change. A series of intensive training sessions was begun, using external and internal trainers to raise the consciousness of the college community. Anthony Carnevale (1982), a widely respected economist, spoke to faculty leaders about the changing world economy and the emerging needs of the United States. He pointed out that to be competitive, workers must be able to think quickly, take authority, and make rapid judgments. The same qualities that will prepare students for this highly skilled work force need to be valued in the educational institutions that prepare them. In the dynamic, swiftly shifting requirements of the new economy, institutions have an obligation to examine their priorities and process.

Several additional strategies for creating a dynamic culture of continuous improvement were identified and implemented over several months to support the conception of revitalization. A senior administrator was designated as a change agent for a period of two years, to work with administrators and faculty. A respected staff member was reassigned to work with staff concerns. The human resources department developed a comprehensive training plan. A series of awards for personal and team accomplishment was established. Each unit was asked to determine improvements in their service and/or product. Frequent meetings between groups of administrators and the president were scheduled. Faculty, staff, and administrators were encouraged to communicate by electronic mail, so that everyone, including the president, was electronically accessible. Discussions of a new governance system started with faculty, and discussions for a new planning process were opened. A committee began to explore a new administrative evaluation system. Retreats were held for learning and sharing experiences. Finally, senior administrators were reminded to model the behaviors of continuous improvement: flexibility, coaching, risk taking, and team-centered activities.

Commitment to Quality: Testing the New Culture. These strategies were in place for only eighteen months when fiscal disaster struck. The state and local county governments announced major revenue shortfalls and a series of budgetary reductions to the Montgomery College. Dire possibilities were discussed, from severely cutting programs to furloughs and termination of faculty and staff. In fiscal year 1991, the college was forced to reduce or defer over a million dollars worth of capital projects and absorb another million dollars of state reductions to the operating budget. Some members of the college community who had previously been silent critics of revitalization now openly questioned the wisdom of committing resources to a "management fad" when dollars were short.

As the economic situation worsened, it became clear that the fiscal crisis at the college provided both danger and opportunity. The new participatory culture of personal empowerment and shared decision making allowed the institution to confront the reality of possible downsizing and reassessment of resources as a community. The president and the board of trustees began a process of collaborative review and analysis to affirm priorities, identify appropriate changes, and recommend reallocation of current and projected resources.

This process, which eventually spanned two years, began with across-the-board budget cuts of 10 percent to each college unit. Units were instructed to identify cuts while safeguarding the central mission of the college: the teaching/learning process. Each unit evaluated budgets and volunteered reductions of unit choice up to 10 percent. Positions, equipment, travel, professional development, training, and other activities were evaluated for reduction.

The board of trustees held a day-long open hearing to listen to the college and community as they brought forth concerns about the reductions and suggestions for lowering expenditures and enhancing revenues. The entire college community as well as groups such as the faculty congress, the staff senate, and the administrative team were asked to provide suggestions either at the hearing or in writing to the board. Over one hundred suggestions were eventually received, reviewed, and distilled into forty-five distinct alternatives. The president and the cabinet developed work groups to research the suggestions and arrive at a position statement to address each one. An all-day retreat of 150 faculty and staff leaders was called to obtain feedback on these positions. The position statements, as well as the group comments, were distributed for additional feedback to the entire college.

The cabinet then reviewed the positions and college-wide input and recommended a course of action on each alternative to the board of trustees. At a final open hearing, the board accepted fourteen suggestions for immediate implementation and another eighteen for further study, and it decided against thirteen. The new culture of open communication, cooperation, and shared values had made it possible for the institution to make changes which would have been divisive and loudly denounced in another era. The crisis had provided the opportunity to assess priorities and make changes in staffing, programs, and procedures.

Out of eleven hundred staff positions, sixteen were eliminated and another thirty were reallocated. Programs and services were evaluated, fees instituted, benefits adjusted, and support systems downsized. However, not one faculty position was eliminated, not one healthy academic program was suspended, and not one employee was terminated. The college community had participated intensively in a stressful process that ultimately left the college lean, healthy, and rededicated to the mission of teaching, learning, and student success.

The Mission Is the Message

Growth is inevitable; the alternative is death or atrophy. An institution conceived to meet community needs must continue to change as the environment changes. To understand the impact of growth and structure on the organization, it is necessary to relate both process and structure to an underlying philosophy. Each community college has a vision and mission. The mission is successful if information is developed to determine relative success and the basis for improvement.

Mission, vision, and direction must be in congruence to achieve continuous improvement. Only the people who make up the organization can bring these into harmony. Individual employees need to feel that their contributions are important and make a difference. True empowerment occurs when instructors and staff take full ownership of their jobs and begin to evaluate themselves and their performance. If the prevailing ethic promotes a cycle of self-knowledge, self-evaluation, and personal responsibility, improvement will occur. In such a system, employees use evaluation and review to determine success (congruence of mission, vision, direction) and redirect if necessary. Evaluation is used to facilitate continuous improvement. This is true quality management, and it can be achieved only when people are made to feel their power within the organization and then use this power to further the vision and mission of the institution.

These factors can give community colleges a competitive edge in training workers for a worldwide economy. An enlightened staff consisting of people committed to continuous improvement and excellence will make the difference in institutional winners and losers. Continuous improvement, ownership, empowerment, and constant self-evaluation will build a cycle of success for community colleges and replenish the energy and optimism of their early days of development.

References

Adelman, C. Women at Thirtysomething: Paradoxes of Attainment. Washington, D.C.: U.S. Department of Education, 1991.

Adelman, C. The Community College as American Thermometer. Washington, D.C.: U.S. Department of Education, 1992.

Carnevale, A. P. America and the New Economy. San Francisco: Jossey-Bass, 1982.

Cohen, A. M., and Brawer, F. B. The American Community College. San Francisco: Jossey-Bass, 1989.

Garreau, J. "Where the Voters Are: In America's Changing, Burgeoning Suburbia, from Mall to Shining Mall." Washington Post, Aug. 2, 1992, p. C2.

Peters, T. J., and Waterman, R. H. In Search of Excellence. New York: HarperCollins, 1982.

Tuttle, T. "What Is Total Quality?" The Maryland Workplace, Winter 1989, p. 4.

ROBERT E. PARILLA is president of Montgomery College in Rockville, Maryland.

*Canadore College's Associates Model of Governance views hierarchy
as a value-added process rather than a compliance control structure.*

From Boxing to Ballet:
Remaking a Community College

Garth Jackson, Nancy Moulton

The mid 1980s were a time of growth and development in the province of
Ontario. As the decade came to a close, the federal government concluded its
free trade discussions with the United States with the signing of the Free Trade
Agreement. Significant economic adjustment occurred, with offices closing and
hundreds of people becoming unemployed. Shortly thereafter, the federal government imposed a general sales tax on most goods and services in Canada.
With the application of this new federal tax and the Free Trade Agreement, a
number of businesses, particularly in manufacturing, closed offices in Canada
and relocated in the United States where labor and transportation were perceived to be cheaper. Ontario, as the major manufacturing center for the country, was significantly affected by these events. As businesses closed and
thousands of people joined the ranks of the unemployed, the costs for social
support systems rose dramatically, provincial expenditures increased significantly, and provincial tax revenue decreased dramatically.

In two-year colleges, senior administrators were attempting to cope with
entirely new problems. Government support in the form of transfer payments,
which had previously increased at a nominal rate, were dramatically reduced,
whereas expenditures continued to increase as a result of new social legisla-
tion, larger benefit and pension contributions, and escalating demands for
postsecondary and skill training. The real dollar value of the transfer payments
was quickly decreasing. As government became more aware of its financial
realities, colleges were informed that transfer payments would be frozen and,
indeed, current funding levels would be reduced.

This crisis of reduced funding and increased demand left colleges with no
choice but to make deep expenditure reductions in an alarmingly short period

of time. Cuts of this type defy all normal rules of consultation and leave in their wake administrators harboring concerns about the quality of education and stress in the work environment and faculty and support staff feeling removed from decision making. Over time, it becomes obvious that the old way of doing business must change. Creative solutions require input from support staff and faculty as well as the consumers—the students.

Governance in Transition

Nineteen Colleges of Applied Arts and Technology (CAATs) were established twenty-five years ago in Ontario "to provide courses of types and levels beyond, or not suited to, the secondary school setting; to meet the needs of graduates from any secondary school program, apart from those wishing to attend university; and, to meet the educational needs of adults and out-of-school youth, whether or not they are secondary school graduates" (Ontario Department of Education, p. 13). At the time, North Bay, a city of approximately fifty thousand people, became home to one of the Northern Ontario satellite campuses. Within five years, the campus separated from its parent Institution, and Canadore College became an independent CAAT.

The CAATs were unique in that each was governed by its own board of governors consisting of twelve appointed volunteers, and every academic program had an advisory committee of career practitioners appointed by and reporting to the board. In turn, the advisory body to government, the Ontario Council of Regents, provided recommendations to the appropriate provincial minister and recommended the appointment of all members of boards. In addition to other responsibilities, the Council of Regents maintained a central negotiating role in collective bargaining with the academic and support staff unions of each college and in the creation and terms and conditions for employment of administrative staff.

Canadore, like most other colleges established during the late 1960s and early 1970s, operated with a normal top-down hierarchical structure common to the "growth" businesses of the time. Early in the college's development, the founding president realized that these new postsecondary institutions must establish their legitimacy within the community and province. Under his guidance and direction, highly skilled faculty and staff were hired; students acquired a high level of skill and knowledge and quickly found employment after graduation; attractive facilities were built, instilling a sense of pride in the institution; and a strong camaraderie developed as staff flourished in this environment and worked collectively for the good of students. Enrollment grew and resulted in two major additions to the main campus and the acquisition of a large centrally located facility that would later become the technology center.

In 1990, the election of a new government in Ontario provided the opportunity to develop a new agenda for faculty and staff. The new government focused on social issues such as equity and diversity while dealing with the demand for a restructured economy. Shifting employment patterns in Ontario made lifelong learning and college access a high priority with government. As the population became more mobile in its search for employment, the need for recognized standards within the colleges became apparent. Immigrant population increased and a large number of mature adults enrolled in the colleges, causing the need for prior learning assessment to be addressed. To ensure that all within the population had the opportunity to become contributing members of society, underrepresented groups were targeted. The government's focus on these groups—women, natives, francophones, those with special needs, and visible minorities—provided the impetus for a revisioning of the colleges' future. The CAATs were to become instruments of public policy; as policy shifted, colleges were to respond accordingly.

At Canadore College this change signaled a need to move in new directions. It become apparent that the board of governors had to become more involved with shaping the college vision. In the late 1980s, four internally elected candidates were added to the college board, increasing membership to sixteen. As the college altered the context for governance, the board enhanced its opportunities to meet with the students and staff. Staff began to attend board committee meetings regularly, and a variety of committees, consisting of representatives from all constituent groups, started to meet with the board prior to its regular monthly meeting.

Legacies of Top-Down Management

Internally, faculty and support staff had to be prepared for the opportunity and responsibilities of shared governance. During fall 1990 senior administrators of the college met with approximately one-third of the college employees. Small groups of ten to fifteen, representing all constituent groups, informally provided their thoughts on the college's future. During this process of information gathering, many comments about input by staff and the lack of direct response by administration were heard. It was decided that three representatives from each group would meet with senior administrators to receive and discuss results of the meetings. A brief summary of the results follows.

Organization. The college was perceived to be disintegrated, competitive, territorial, and isolated. Mandates for committees were often unknown or unclear. The need for a forum for corporate information sharing and decision making, other than the Executive Management Committee, was identified. It was suggested that the college remove invisible walls in an attempt to work better together.

Financial resources. Concern was expressed that budget decisions were made with little or no consultation with appropriate groups and that in some cases financial information was not shared even among managers. Suggestions for new initiatives appeared to be stifled or filed in a "black hole." Staff expressed interest in participating in budget creation and becoming more informed regarding the financial realities of the college.

Marketing and recruitment. While administrators had developed a marketing plan, this information had not been discussed with the college as a whole. Those who were aware of the plan felt that it was not focused on college programs. In cases where administrators had identified targets, many were not communicated to the appropriate personnel. Faculty expressed keen interest and desire in becoming more involved in student recruitment.

Community. It became apparent that the college did not have a clear plan with respect to its relationship with the external community. It was highly regarded but needed to integrate its efforts with those of the community.

Communication. Staff did not articulate a sense of shared mission or direction. Many claimed isolation from one another. A need for a coordinated effort to share information as well as institutional goals and values was identified.

Service. While most of the service areas were providing quality service, many persons felt that the service they received was inadequate and not aligned with user needs. Generally, service areas wanted to provide good service; however, they tended to be driven by the availability of resources. A number of areas had not been challenged to clarify their service focus.

College mission. Unaware of the college's mission statement, many staff created a personal mission for their area of expertise. Although these personal missions supported the college's mission and goals, a clear need arose to revisit the mission and communicate it to the college as a whole.

Human resources. Some suggested that the college's approach to professional development, orientation, and training for all college staff needed to be reviewed. There appeared to be a lack of recognition for a job well done. Staff also expressed a need for a college-wide policy for professional and personal growth for all employees.

Curriculum. A number of curriculum issues were raised. Needs such as the granting of credit for prior learning experience, increasing the number of cooperative education programs, and developing a framework for lifelong learning were identified.

In summary, a number of common themes were voiced by faculty and staff. A lack of trust on the part of college employees was evident, as were a sense of isolation and a feeling that work was not valued and creativity not encouraged or rewarded. Most employees had little or no concept of who their customers really were.

From Boxing to Ballet

In studying faculty and staff perceptions of work life in Canadore College and sharing information widely, our goal was to reduce the size of the "black hole" in governance. We wanted to dance rather than box. The College Council was restructured to provide academic advice to the Office of the President. While the original College Council had a membership of approximately seventy people and met three times a year, the newly structured council consisted of twenty-four members—eight students, eight faculty, four administrators, and four support staff, each elected by his or her constituent group. The council now meets a minimum of ten times during the year.

In response to the issues raised by staff, we presented an Associates Model for Governance to the board of governors for consideration. The goal of this model was to move the college, as our staff perceived the challenge, from one of anxiety, adolescence, compliance, and control to that of adventure, adulthood, accountability, and partnership. Organization development theorists helped provide the foundation through writings that showed positive linkages between people and business when people feel involved in the business.

Canadore College, in many ways, is a collection of people who have chosen to work in the business of education as opposed to other businesses where their skills are equally applicable. The most important link is the link between people and business. To this, people bring qualifications, experience, professional skill, capacity, potential, and most of all motivation. But a reality that profoundly impacts this connection or link is the fact that the business does not remain static. Because business changes as economic and social variables affect it, it is important to constantly monitor it, refine it, and adjust it. Community college business is different from secondary, university, or private trade school education. As an instrument of public policy, community college business by definition will change as public policy shifts.

The purpose of organization is to create a positive working environment, reflect the changing nature of business for all staff, and feed, nurture and encourage each of us so that the people–business link is the strongest possible. In this view, organization is clearly organic rather than static, and the aim of the organization is to create opportunities for achieving greater staff potential, encourage morale, and then get out of the way.

The top-down hierarchical organization that Canadore College used to make decisions and get work done was an organization that got in the way of staff. Because of obvious problems associated with an organization of this type—one that precludes or denies staff involvement—a natural temptation arises to choose a different hierarchical configuration—that is, to move boxes around to solve the problem. We resisted this temptation on the basis that changing the number of boxes or incumbents would have short-term value but no long-term effects. Regardless of the number of boxes and layers in an organization's hierarchy, a compliance control structure persists.

The Associates Model for Governance we presented to the board of governance is a significant and very different way of viewing the organization. Canadore has moved toward a view of hierarchy as a value-added process rather than a compliance control structure. Reflecting on our reality, we decided to avoid hierarchy and use instead a template elaborated by Ricardo Semler in his article "Managing Without Managers" (1989) (see Figure 3.1).

Figure 3.1. The Associates' Model for Governance

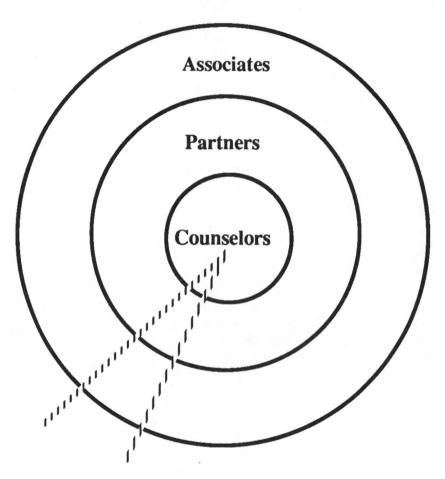

In this view, the role of partners (administrators) is to add value to the work of the institution, which is really the work of the associates (faculty and staff). The role of the counselors (board and president) is to add value through high-performance counseling of all within the college. Essentially this model moves beyond organizational values of the past—compliance, control, and loyalty—to organizational values of the future—trust, participation, partnership, recognition, innovation, creativity, client service, and student success.

Some changes are immediately apparent when the organization is viewed this way. Policy work, proposals, projects, and so on, cannot proceed to completion without majority impact from associates. Hiring and recruitment cannot be undertaken without majority impact on decisions from the appropriate constituent group. Planning the academic year becomes an associate-based activity facilitated by partners. Professional development, skills training for staff, and organizational development assume a high priority.

To make this change work, three principles must be recognized: (1) the mission must be clear, (2) the values on which performance is based must be clear, and (3) information critical to decision making must be timely and fully shared.

Testing the Model

While this model was substantially different from that which had been used historically at Canadore College, staff expressed interest in participating and becoming more involved. The challenge to change the culture of the institution rather than the "boxes on an organizational chart" was generally agreed to be worth everyone's effort.

Testing the model, in the real world of diminishing finances, changing government policies, and increasing consumer demands is another story. The new model was immediately put to work through a number of partnering activities:

• To respond to pressing financial concerns, a Union–Management Finance Committee, consisting of equal representation from both unions and management, was created. While participating in current budget decisions, this committee began planning its activities to respond to significant budget reductions in the following year. As part of its planning strategy, the committee invited input from the college community. A total of 142 expenditure reduction recommendations were provided by staff. All recommendations were recorded, reviewed, and the vast majority implemented.

• A Partners' Forum, consisting of deans, directors, and senior administrators and those having institutional responsibilities (i.e., the chairs of the College Council and the Education and Employment Equity Committee), was formed and convenes twice a month. This forum provides an opportunity to share information informally and review options for addressing corporate issues.

• A Student Success Committee, composed of representatives from all constituent groups, was established to respond to the college's high rate of attrition. The committee meets regularly and reports to the Office of the President on a continual basis. As might be expected, one of their major findings was that students were leaving college because of financial problems. As a result, the Emergency Student Loan Fund was immediately doubled to respond to this short-term financial need.

• Service Advisory Committees were established for all service areas in the college. These committees, consisting of representatives from all constituent groups, meet a minimum of three times a year. Members provide advice and assistance to the service area, helping to focus action, and provide feedback on quality performance.

• Professional development at the college has become a strategic priority as demonstrated by an increase in the allocation of resources. Departments have assumed responsibility for the activity within their own areas, and a Central Professional Development Committee was formed to ensure that college-wide activities occur regularly.

• The weekly Executive Management Committee meetings were suspended, and short daily meetings are held instead with the vice presidents. This nucleus has become known as the Office of the President. Staff members are invited to meet with the Office of the President informally at any time to discuss any topic requiring immediate action.

During the past three years, a number of position papers have been forwarded to the college for its review and comment. Papers that may have a significant effect on the college as a whole are reviewed by task groups consisting of members from all constituent groups. While this becomes a time-consuming task, in subsequent discussions and policy development, the college is more informed, aware of the issues, and can draw from a pool of in-house experts.

On a broader scale, the college has acted as a broker for the community in developing and submitting proposals for community projects. While there may be limited financial contribution to the college in organizing and participating in these projects, the resultant goodwill and networking are significant. The college has taken on a legitimate role as a community partner in local social and economic development.

The college is attempting to determine its effectiveness as it begins the second phase of a three-year operational review. Rather than a special team designated to conduct operational review, the majority of the review will be done by in-house Service Advisory Committees. The theme for the review, "Customer Service," was selected by the entire college community. The operational review steering committee, consisting of representatives from all constituent groups as well as an external advisory group, identified four areas of concern associated with customer service: access, planning, innovation and creativity, and evaluation and monitoring. Questions for review were formulated by the steering committee. A special review team, consisting of a member of the Board of Governors, the presidents of both unions, the Student Representative Council, and the Administrative Association, as well as the operational review steering committee's external advisor, will review the performance of the Board of Governors and the Office of the President. The president participates as a resource person on the team. The College Council will be a prime participant in the academic review. While this review differs from previous ones, it reflects the current climate of the college and involves all constituent groups.

Looking at the Bottom Line

As the college has moved forward with its Associates Model for Governance, a number of bottom lines have surfaced that may be useful to institutions considering a similar change in their approach to governance. The role of the Governing Board will need to change from monitoring to policy setting, playing the advocate role, and creating a vision for the college in service of the community. Institutions considering implementing such a model should recognize that, in their efforts to include faculty and support staff, they must not forget the contribution of administrators must not be forgotten. Recently, an administrative association was created at our college; it should have been considered much earlier in the process. While both unions and the students selected members to sit on various committees, administrators, who may have attended meetings as resource individuals, often also assumed the role of representing the administrative staff. Little accountability to the remaining administrative group was the result.

Unlike faculty, participation in committees is a new experience for staff and students. There is a need to provide training to all participants on chairing meetings, sharing information, and becoming effective committee members. A review of the committee membership indicates that a limited number of people sit on numerous committees and actively participate in the decision making of the college. Others need to be encouraged to participate so that they can add value to the decisions being made. While students undertake to represent their constituent group on various committees, they often find they are unable to attend because of onerous academic and work commitments. If students are to become full participants in the governance of the college, then issues of learning, application, and credit for involvement must be addressed. Members of the Board of Governors also need to acquire skills in meeting with other boards. This effort takes time and planning but is of utmost importance if the invited guests are to feel that their contribution is valued.

When shifts occur in the culture of the institution, staff should be made aware of these changes. Historically, many Canadore employees felt that to identify oneself with labor meant that one was antimanagement. Conversely, many felt that a lack of involvement in the union demonstrated one's support for management. However, in the current environment, active involvement in unions leads to participation in the decision making of the college. This cultural change must be clearly communicated early in the process. The opportunity for union members to become more involved in the decision making of the college elicited mixed feelings by a significant number of union members. Those who were actively involved were generally pleased and excited; those who tended to be nonparticipants appeared skeptical and concerned. The important lesson is that open communication early in the process would have led to involvement of more people.

To provide support and encourage participation, goodwill ambassadors should be cultivated within each department or division. These ambassadors, while having the support of their union or association, should be comfortable communicating with all constituent groups. Even though an employee assistance plan is in place at the college, many employees and students feel the need to meet with someone with whom they can quickly confide and seek advice. The goodwill ambassadors can encourage fellow employees to play a larger role in the decision making of the college. These ambassadors could provide a much-needed short-term service and facilitate increased trust and respect among faculty and staff. They would not deter from the union's participation but act as mentors within the college and a support for the union.

How successful has Canadore College been with the Associates Model of Governance? During the past three years, the college has reduced its budget by almost $6 million and increased its enrollment by 22 to 25 percent. Members of the college are more active in their unions, and administrators have formed an association to address issues related to their management role. Students are participating in decisions affecting their future, and governors are setting policies for the college and determining its future direction. Two probationary faculty members won excellent teacher awards for their divisions during the past year. The students, in consultation with the college's alumni, have received board approval to begin construction of a student center. The most recent evidence of the model's success can be seen in the college's operating budget—the staff complement was decreased by a total of seventy-four full-time equivalent positions without any imposed layoffs.

It appears that the Associates Model is being accepted and becoming more effective and efficient. However, we, as participants, must be cautious that we do not become complacent and accept the model without examining its effectiveness or trying to improve it. This model takes time, commitment, energy, and participation, making for a challenging, exciting, and productive undertaking. With strong commitment demonstrated daily by all constituent groups, we are confident that the Associates Model will continue to move Canadore College forward as it endeavors to achieve excellence.

References

Ontario Department of Education. Colleges of Applied Arts and Technology—Basic Documents. Toronto: Ontario Department of Education, 1967.

Pitman, W. The Report of the Advisor to the Minister of Colleges and Universities on the Governance of the Colleges of Applied Arts and Technology. Toronto, Ontario: Ministry of Colleges and Universities, 1986.

Semler, R. "Managing Without Managers." Harvard Business Review, Sept.–Oct. 1989, pp. 76–84.

GARTH JACKSON is president of Canadore College of Applied Arts and Technology in North Bay, Ontario, Canada.

NANCY MOULTON is assistant to the president at Canadore College.

PART TWO

Changing Management Roles
and Responsibilities

*If managing effectively in an age of uncertainty will require plan-
ning and leading fundamental change, then change should begin
with the development of a new planning model.*

Managing Uncertainty:
Thinking and Planning Strategically

Albert L. Lorenzo

As the end of the twentieth century approaches, we are being told to expect an
environment of extreme uncertainty. In fact, "organizational environments are
now so turbulent that the notion that an organization can do in the future what
it has done in the past makes sense to very few people, if any at all" (Ziegenfuss, 1989, p. 179). What we do know, however, is that the growing turbulence is a direct result of the continual interaction of forces of rapid and radical
change.

Rapid change refers to the ever-increasing pace of change. Even though the
direction of rapid change is somewhat predictable, its speed is sometimes over-
whelming. In order to accommodate rapid change, organizations are typically
challenged to run faster and work harder. While this strategy works for a while,
an organization will ultimately reach the upper limit of its ability to move more
quickly.

Radical change is much more dramatic. It is less linear, more abrupt, and
less predictable. It frequently brings about a change in the rules or the way in
which things are being done. Moving faster will not accommodate radical
change. Rather, it requires an organization to work smarter by continually
learning and developing new methods and models.

Based on what is known about the nature of these two forces, it would
appear that the best strategy for accommodating the turbulence caused by
rapid and radical change is a form of change itself—fundamental change. The
term *fundamental change* refers to a modification of the organization's foundation or core practices and beliefs. Fundamental change lays new groundwork
and produces new guiding principles. It actually changes the essence of the
organization.

New Directions for Community Colleges, no. 84, Winter 1993 © Jossey-Bass Publishers

Perhaps not coincidentally, the leading management and organizational theorists of the day have chosen an atmospheric metaphor to convey their thinking. The characteristics of massive weather systems, for example, provide a good way of describing the current organizational context.

Consider a hurricane. Forecasters can know that conditions are right for such a storm but may not be able to predict its timing. Even after the storm develops, it is not always possible to predict its ultimate wind velocity, much less its direction. Sometimes storms turn inland, causing massive destruction. Other times, they move out to sea and are barely remembered.

Tornadoes provide another insight. They develop suddenly, sometimes following conditions that might cause us to expect a different outcome. Their direction and duration are unpredictable. They also have a strange tendency to touch down in random patterns, destroying several homes yet sparing many others in the same neighborhood.

Whether the anticipated disturbance is a storm in the atmospheric environment or growing turbulence in the organizational environment, the strategy of choice is sound planning. But if managing effectively in an environment of turbulence and uncertainty requires leading and implementing fundamental change, then the first fundamental change organizations should make is in the way they plan.

This chapter will focus on identifying the emerging requirements for organizational planning in an age of uncertainty, particularly as they relate to our nation's twelve hundred community colleges. It will use the concept of systems theory as a framework for developing a new perspective on an organization, and it will propose a new model designed to guide two-year colleges in thinking and planning strategically.

Evolution of Planning Models

The ways in which organizations plan have typically reflected the conditions of the times. Following World War II, for example, corporate planning was primarily an internally focused process. The organization looked almost exclusively at itself—its products, people, resources, and markets—and then made a decision as to which course of action to pursue.

This inside-out approach worked well primarily because the United States was in a rather unique economic position. The war had destroyed or seriously damaged the productive capacity of most of the rest of the industrialized world. There were pent-up consumer demands, especially for capital goods, and a birthrate unparalleled in U.S. history. Economic activity was brisk, natural resources were plentiful, demand was strong, and the potential for growth seemed unlimited. The only constraints on organizational action appeared to be those that an organization chose to place on itself.

By the 1960s, however, things began to change. Other nations had rebuilt their productive capacity and were bringing products to market in direct competition with American goods. Demographically, the postwar baby boom came to an end in 1964. The regulatory practices of governmental units began to escalate, and the first of many civil and human rights laws were enacted. In short, the 1960s marked an end to the era of organizational self-determination, as factors external to the organization began to mandate change.

The growing impact of conditions external to the organization meant that the models previously used for planning had to change. No longer could a company look exclusively inside itself to choose a direction. The challenge was simultaneously to assess both internal and external conditions and merge the findings into a single set of options. The model that ultimately accommodated this need came to be known as strategic planning.

The shift to a strategic planning model brought numerous benefits. Organizations were able to ensure a better fit between themselves and their markets. More business opportunities were uncovered, and external threats could be anticipated further in advance. More importantly, the organization was better positioned to assess the need for change and monitor the potential for resource fluctuations.

Although the concept of strategic planning is widely assumed to have started in the business community during the 1960s, it took until the early 1980s for the practice to be used in higher education (Cope, 1987). The lag is probably explained by the fact that colleges and universities, by design, were intended to operate somewhat more removed from their external environments. But as harsh economic, demographic, and political realities began to permeate the academic veil, the majority of collegiate institutions began making the shift to a strategic planning approach.

The strategic planning models typically used in higher education have been virtually identical to those used in business. Both begin with a predetermined statement of mission and then proceed to a simultaneous assessment of internal and external conditions. Internally, the entity assesses its major strengths and weaknesses. Externally, it scans for environmental opportunities and threats. Evaluating the interrelationship of strengths, weaknesses, opportunities, and threats produces a set of strategic alternatives, from among which a final set of organizational directions are selected.

Baldridge and Okimi (1982) suggest that the central focus of strategic planning in higher education is developing a good fit between the organization's activities and the demands of surrounding environments. They further suggest that strategic planning must look at the big picture: the long-range destiny of the institution, the competition with other organizations in its service environment, the markets for organizational products and services, and the mix of internal resources to accomplish the institution's purpose.

Although the benefits of using a strategic planning model are still apparent, mounting evidence suggests that this approach is beginning to fall short of expectations. Noted management scientist Peter Drucker (1992) has said that uncertainty—in the economy, society, politics—has become so great as to render futile, if not counterproductive, the kind of planning most organizations still practice: forecasting based on probabilities.

Drucker's comments echo those of many corporate CEOs. A survey of corporate executives conducted by the management consulting firm of Harbridge House (American Society of Training and Development, 1990) reports that CEOs still consider strategic planning valuable, but it is no longer the number one management issue. Keeping plans flexible and putting plans into action have become higher priorities.

The Harbridge House survey concludes that fully 81 percent of the executives polled said "increasing flexibility to respond to unforeseen developments" is a major or important organizational priority. Also, 80 percent of the respondents cited a need for "better implementation planning" as a priority, while 71 percent wanted more "built-in flexibility for future conditions." In short, executives agree that "long-range thinking is important, but long-range planning can be a trap" (p. 10).

Given this growing concern about the viability of current planning models in an age of uncertainty, the time may be right for another evolution in model design. But just what changes are needed?

Requirements of a New Age

Drucker (1992), with eloquent simplicity, characterizes one needed change as a shift from basing decisions on "What is most likely to happen?" to asking instead, "What has already happened that will create the future?"

In a more extensive analysis, senior management consultant Ian Wilson (1990) examines the historic underpinnings of the move to strategic planning and how the concept has evolved in the past twenty years. Then, looking to the future, Wilson suggests that to remain effective, strategic planning models must become more holistic by encompassing and integrating more elements. He also believes that they should become more issues oriented. Finally, Wilson states that a new model must incorporate a vision, but in a very pragmatic sense.

Peter Vaill (1989) offers additional insight and explains that the reason some traditional planning models are becoming outmoded is because the contexts surrounding a situation will not hold still long enough to make a planned course of action feasible. He argues that directions and policies can only be temporary and ad hoc, that they can no longer be the timeless benchmarks they once were. Vaill suggests that when it comes to planning in an age of uncertainty and instability, some kind of "guidance system" is needed that might be equally flexible, or at least have the potential of becoming equally flexible.

Another requirement is related to organizational maturity. Organizational life cycle theory suggests that as organizations develop, they pass through a series of readily identifiable phases or life cycle stages. Each stage brings with it a different set of organizational characteristics and needs. Management scientists generally agree on four dominant life cycle phases: birth, growth, maturity, and decline (Quinn and Cameron, 1983). Some identify a fifth stage, renewal, positioned after maturity, that postpones the period of decline.

During each life cycle stage, ongoing organizational viability is pursued through the differing "foundation strategies" illustrated here:

Life Cycle Stage	Foundation Strategy
Birth	Acceptance and recognition
Growth	Accommodating demand
Maturity and renewal	Continuous improvement and continuous adaptation
Decline	Redefinition and restructuring

An effective planning model will provide information and feedback that support the appropriate foundation strategies. For mature organizations, that means facilitating continuous improvement and continuous adaptation.

In summary, then, based on the insights of these organizational theorists and theories, a planning model designed for community colleges in an age of uncertainty will provide a pragmatic vision for the institution and an understanding of the factors creating the future. It will generate a set of strategic issues as well as more traditional strategic options. It will consider the institution both as a system in itself and as a part of larger systems. It will facilitate continuous improvement internally and continuous adaptation to changes occurring externally. And it will do all of this on an ongoing basis.

Shifts in the Strategic Context

Additional requirements for a redefined planning model can be identified by examining certain shifts occurring in the strategic operating context of many community colleges. Four of the more dramatic shifts are summarized next (Banach and Lorenzo, 1993).

Public opinion is having an increasing impact on institutional success. More frequently than ever before, community colleges are being judged in the court of public opinion. Perhaps more than any other contextual factor, the potential impact of adverse public opinion drives the need for a new planning approach. The reason is simple: advanced communication technologies can reinforce or alter public opinion in minutes. Without an effective means to monitor and shape public sentiment, our colleges can find themselves working contrary to the wishes of this ultimate court. Nothing can succeed for long without the sanction of public opinion, especially in the public sector.

Quality and effectiveness are replacing quantity and efficiency as the primary measures of institutional performance. There is more and better competition in the marketplace, and less consumer loyalty. The primary concern today should be to work at getting better before one worries about getting bigger. Much the same is true for cost and price. Offering the cheapest price is no longer any assurance of market share. People are more willing to pay a higher price if it guarantees quality, performance, and convenience.

Employee attitudes are becoming more critical to institutional success. Community colleges will have to help staff appreciate the vision and mission of the institution, and they will have to create a process that allows faculty and staff to express their feelings about the institution. In short, as employees get harder to hire (and fire), effective colleges will work to build staff ownership into the well-being of the organization. They will also invest energy in raising the agenda and broadening the knowledge and skills of employees in an effort to help them become advocates of productive change.

Institutional constituencies are becoming larger in number and more diverse in composition. United Way's issue identification program points to the "mosaic society" as one of the change drivers of the 1990s. As the U.S. population continues to subdivide into smaller clusters, demands for responsive programs and services are likely to escalate. The new mosaic society will also force more community colleges to engage in highly targeted niche marketing.

Requirements for a New Model

Successful approaches to strategic planning and thinking should reflect concepts that are emerging in organizational theory and shifts that are occurring in the strategic context. They should also retain the best of current planning models. Following are some specific requirements for a new model of strategic planning in community colleges.

The planning model should emphasize process over product. Leaders still view planning as a terminal, product-oriented task. Process, however, connotes adaptability and the continual reassessment of organizational direction. In effect, processing becomes a college's ongoing means of monitoring internal operating conditions, scanning for turbulence in the environment, and signaling the need for midcourse corrections. It can also provide assurance that things are on course and going well.

The model must produce a clear sense of purpose and an understanding of relationship to the larger environment. Further, this purpose must be closely aligned with the public interest, especially for public sector organizations such as community colleges. The greater the degree of alignment is between public interest and institutional purpose, the more successful the institution will be in garnering the resources required to pursue its mission and vision.

The model must devote greater attention to measuring effectiveness and improving quality. Once a community college has established a clear understanding of its purpose and instilled in its stakeholders a vision of how that purpose can be achieved, it must have a reality test. It must be able to answer quantitatively whether its performance matches its purpose and whether that purpose is addressing some public need. To the extent that the institution is able to document superior performance in relationship to identified needs, the greater the likelihood that it will continually be able to improve quality and capitalize on radical change.

Faculty and staff attitudes must be monitored systematically and objectively. Institutional climate is an aggregate of employee attitudes, and it can be assessed by measuring factors such as communication, satisfaction, cooperation, decision making, trust, leadership, and collaboration. By acting on the findings of such assessments and monitoring improvements, community college leaders can foster higher levels of employee commitment and enthusiasm, which is central to improving institutional performance.

To determine more accurately the external forces triggering the need for change, community colleges must strengthen their ability to scan both the local and extended environments. The reason, of course, is to identify potential opportunities and threats as early and accurately as possible. The extended scan will identify factors that are having an impact on most organizations, while the local scan will focus on change drivers more unique to the institution itself.

The environmental scan must be designed to reflect the expectations of multiple and diverse constituencies. When assessing needs, community colleges must be sure to include the needs of multiple constituencies. That does not mean that all needs will ultimately be addressed. On the contrary, few colleges will have the capacity in today's economic environment to be all things to all people. But the decision to address certain needs over others must be a conscious decision, one made after considering all of the competing options and opportunities.

The planning model must include a means to monitor and influence public opinion. Regardless of how positive a college's internal effectiveness indicators are, the institution will suffer if the public sees things differently. More than ever before, the perception is the reality. Effective organizations have always monitored public opinion. Now community colleges will need to take the next step and establish a formal process designed to help shape public opinion.

For mature community colleges, the planning model must provide a basis for continuous improvement and continuous adaptation. Mature institutions must continually evolve and improve if they want to avoid drifting into the more risky life cycle stage of decline. Historically, planning processes have emphasized the new, sometimes at the expense of the old. A more contemporary approach would balance innovation with improvement and replacement with adaptation. This more comprehensive view can provide an expanded list of strategic options, and it will help guide a mature college to subsequent periods of renewal instead of decline.

Framing the Planning Model

Although the outward thrust of strategic planning has been a significant improvement over the more linear, internally-focused practice of long-range planning, both approaches have tended to view an organization primarily as an independent, semiautonomous entity. One of the lessons leaders have been taught by the forces of change affecting our institutions is how interrelated and interdependent organizations really are.

This connectedness is being observed on two levels simultaneously. Internally, a change in one division or unit can have broad implications throughout the institution. Externally, even a change occurring halfway around the world can ultimately force change in a community college in a particular service region. These conditions challenge a fundamental assumption used in previous planning models: the independence and autonomy of the college. This situation is probably what has prompted Wilson's call for a "more holistic" approach to strategic planning.

A body of knowledge that can aid in understanding interrelationships is systems theory. Myers (1992) defines systems theory quite succinctly by stating, "Every level of our existence is composed of subsystems and is itself a subcomponent of a larger system" (p. 511). Myers concludes that in order to understand one system, one must know how it interacts with other systems and subsystems.

Recently, a number of organizational theorists have suggested the use of systems theory and its derivative, systems thinking, in organizational planning. In one of the more prominent works on the subject of systems thinking, The Fifth Discipline, MIT's Peter Senge (1990) laments, "From a very early age we are taught to break apart problems, to fragment the world. This apparently makes complex tasks and subjects more manageable, but we pay a hidden enormous price. We can no longer see the consequences of our actions; we lose our intrinsic sense of connection to a larger whole" (p. 3).

Senge defines systems thinking as a discipline for seeing wholes. He presents it as a framework for seeing interrelationships among things and patterns of change rather than static "snapshots." He argues, "Today, systems thinking is needed more than ever because we are being overwhelmed by complexity. Systems thinking is a discipline for seeing the 'structures' that underlie complex situations" (p. 69).

Two of the most recent works to echo Senge's ideas are from Mitroff and Linstone (1993) and Lynch (1993). Mitroff and Linstone describe "New Thinking," which involves unbounded systems thinking in which every one of the sciences and professions is considered fundamental to planning and problem solving. They believe that planners will have made the ultimate transition in perspective when they see the world as an interconnected whole.

Lynch focuses more directly on leadership in the public and nonprofit sectors. He suggests that in order to bring out the best in their organizations, leaders will have to see the future as something to create, that only through people will new things happen, and that leaders must proactively think in terms of the whole system.

Given such high praise for the value of systems thinking in planning organizational futures, it would logically follow that any new planning model should at least consider this emerging discipline. Possibly the basic principles of systems theory might be helpful in framing a new planning model.

In the broadest terms, all systems are classified into two categories: open systems and closed systems. According to Waddington (1978), "A closed system consists of a series of interacting processes which operate inside an impenetrable envelope. Nothing relevant to the operation of the processes can come into the system from the outside, or go from the system to the outside through the envelope" (p. 333). He notes that such systems are rare in practice.

Waddington points out that in contrast to closed systems, "In an open system there is no impenetrable envelope; things important to the actions of the system can come in and go out again" (p. 333). According to these definitions, community colleges should be viewed as open systems.

There are also three separate types of systems. According to Waddington, a mechanistic system is one in which the rules of operation are laid down from the beginning and are not altered regardless of the change in external circumstances. An adaptive system is one that possesses some way of altering its internal behavior in response to the environment in which it exists. Finally, there is a purposive system involving entities that can formulate purposes and act to achieve them. Given these distinctions, community colleges operating in the public or nonprofit sector should be viewed as both adaptive and purposive systems.

A final insight from systems theory to help frame a new perspective for community college planning is the relative position of organizations among the various levels of systems. While theorists disagree as to the ability to define precisely and defend a specific number of systemic levels, the framework for living systems proposed by James Miller (1978) is particularly valuable in organizational understanding.

Miller proposes a hierarchy of seven levels, with each higher level consisting of assemblies of systems at the next lower level. The seven levels are the cell, the organ, the organism, the group, the organization, society, and the supranational system. Miller's central thesis is that systems at all levels are open systems, composed of subsystems that process inputs, throughputs, and outputs of various forms of matter, energy, and information.

Since systems will be interacting most frequently with the systems immediately above and below them, by applying Miller's hierarchy to organizational activity, we should view a community college first as an assembly of a varying number of groups and second as a subsystem of a particular service area society. An extension of Miller's thesis would suggest that the system at each level of the hierarchy is dependent on the systems below for its functioning and that it exists to serve the needs of the systems above it.

By merging the insights gained from systems theory, we can reframe our perspective of an organization from that of an independent, semiautonomous entity to one of an open, adaptive, and purposive system, dependent on the performance of its subgroups for effective functioning, and existing to further the purposes of the society of which it is a part. Applied to community colleges, we can view the institution as a flexible, adaptive organization dependent on the commitment of its faculty and staff for effective performance and existing to meet the needs of constituencies in its service region.

Strategic Guidance Model for Planning and Thinking

Having reframed the concept of an organization from that of an entity to a system, Vaill's earlier reference to a "guidance system" hints at an analogy that may be helpful in visualizing the characteristics of the model being sought. Prior to take-off, a commercial pilot is expected to file a rather detailed flight plan. The plan indicates the destination and outlines anticipated aspects of the trip, such as course headings, speed, and altitude. The flight plan considers the characteristics of the aircraft as well as the condition of the environment through which the plane is expected to travel.

But regardless of the level of detail considered in the preflight planning, once airborne, the original plan will probably not be followed to the letter. On-board guidance systems constantly monitor the condition of the aircraft (internal factors) and the nature of the environment (external factors); they provide the pilot with indications of when a deviation from the original plan should be initiated. Guidance systems are also process-oriented; that is, information and feedback are provided continually, not just periodically.

In today's turbulent and ever-changing environment, it is no more likely that a community college will achieve its long-term goals than an airliner will arrive at its predetermined destination, unless frequent midcourse corrections are made. Accordingly, a planning model designed for community colleges in an age of uncertainty should not only provide a specific initial plan of action but also continually monitor the need to update and correct it.

Figure 4.1 illustrates a proposed Strategic Guidance Model. It blends both old and new concepts to accommodate an environment of uncertainty and the impacts of rapid and radical change. When the model is applied in a community college, the process begins with the formation of a strategic vision. The vision must set forth and clarify the fundamental purpose of the institution. That purpose, in turn, is reexpressed in the form of a specific mission statement. From this central point, the strategic guidance model splits into simultaneous internal and external assessment components.

Questions of quality, employee attitudes (climate), and overall performance are addressed on the organizational assessment (internal) side of the model. The assessment process should include subjective measures (for example, individual perceptions) as well as more objective indicators (for example,

Figure 4.1. Strategic Guidance Model

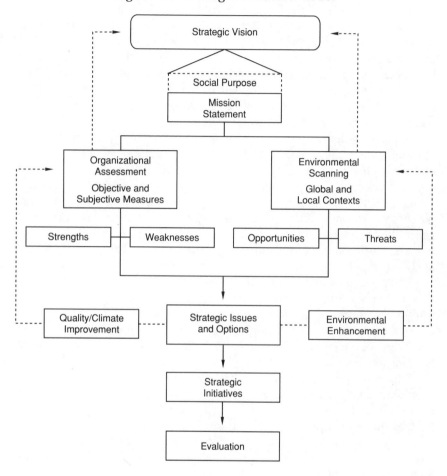

student outcomes, cost, and so on) of actual performance. The goals associated with this side of the model include creating an ongoing process for assessing institutional effectiveness, identifying the specific strengths and weaknesses
of the enterprise, assessing organizational climate, and facilitating the foundation strategy of continuous improvement.

Questions of contextual change, public opinion, and programmatic need
are addressed on the environmental scanning (external) side of the model. The
scan should include indicators of momentum in both the global and local operating contexts, since both can trigger the need for change in institutional strategy. The scan must also be designed to reflect the needs of diverse constituencies. The goals associated with this side of the model include creating a process
that signals the need to adjust programs and services, identifying specific

opportunities and threats to the institution, monitoring and influencing public opinion, and facilitating the foundation strategy of continuous adaptation.

Careful analysis and comparison of institutional strengths and weaknesses with environmental opportunities and threats will generate a series of strategic issues and options. Strategic options are defined as those alternatives that hold potential for institutional advancement and can be initiated quickly. They are usually characterized by an immediate match between an environmental opportunity and an institutional strength. Decision making is generally limited to questions of whether or when to move ahead.

Strategic issues, on the other hand, are matters that warrant institutional attention but typically come to the forefront without the benefit of a clear strategy or direction. In fact, strategic issues will likely be surrounded by widely differing opinions as to their relevancy and intensity and, most frequently, by disagreement as to the appropriate actions to be taken. Unlike the more visible choices associated with strategic options, responses to strategic issues must generally be developed through dialogue and consensus among key stakeholders. During times of radical change, the Strategic Guidance Model will likely generate far more strategic issues than options.

Once a strategic issue or option has been identified, three alternative actions can be taken: launch a strategic initiative, strengthen the institution through a process of quality or climate improvement, and/or improve the external operating context through a process of environmental enhancement. Regardless of the strategy selected, a front-end commitment to evaluation of the decision must be made.

Finally, the information and feedback produced on both sides of the model should ultimately lead to a redefined vision for the institution. Refinements in that vision will provide the basis for institutional renewal and will launch a subsequent wave of process activity through the model.

Looked at in its entirety, the proposed Strategic Guidance Model is actually a system consisting of five major subprocesses that need to be implemented in a community college:

A strategic visioning process that produces a realistic, attractive and future-oriented picture for the college and clearly articulates the social purposes for which the college exists and the specific mission it intends to fulfill

An organizational assessment process designed to determine the institution's overall performance by assessing objective and subjective indicators of strengths and weaknesses in levels of quality, effectiveness, and human resource climate

An environmental scanning process designed to suggest the optimum program–service mix by monitoring changes in both the local and global operating contexts, assessing public opinion, and identifying as early as possible any opportunities or threats to the institution

A quality or climate improvement process intended to facilitate the foundation
  strategy of continuous improvement, rectify any identified weaknesses,
  and enhance the institution's ability to capitalize on environmental opportunities
An environmental enhancement process designed to minimize external threats to
  the institution, showcase the inherent strengths of the enterprise, and facilitate the foundation strategy of continuous adaptation

While traditional long-range and strategic planning models have provided
organizational direction, both were designed to end with a product—the plan.
Once the product was developed, the process typically stopped. But in an age
characterized by rapid and radical change, the emphasis must shift to an ongoing process in community colleges—planning and thinking strategically.

The move to a new model for thinking and planning might help change
our perspective of community colleges as independent and semiautonomous
organizations to open, adaptive, and purposive systems. Just as the strategic
planning model improved on the former long-range planning models by considering factors external to the organization, the Strategic Guidance Model
improves on strategic planning by considering connections and interrelationships.

If managing effectively in an age of uncertainty will require planning and
leading fundamental change, then change should begin with the development
of a new planning model.

References

American Society of Training and Development. "Quick Response Beats Long-Term Planning."
  Training and Development Journal, Oct. 1990, pp. 9–10.
Baldridge, J. V., and Okimi, P. H. "Strategic Planning in Higher Education: New Tool—or New
  Gimmick?" AAHE Bulletin, Oct. 1982, pp. 6, 15–18.
Banach, W. J., and Lorenzo, A. L. Toward a New Model for Thinking and Planning. Warren, Mich.:
  Macomb, 1993.
Cope, R. G. Opportunity from Strength: Strategic Planning Clarified with Case Examples. ASHE-ERIC
  Higher Education Reports, no. 8. Washington, D.C.: Association for the Study of Higher Edu-
  cation, 1987.
Drucker, P. J. "Planning for Uncertainty." Wall Street Journal, July 22, 1992, p. A12.
Lynch, R. LEAD! How Public and Nonprofit Managers Can Bring Out the Best in Themselves and Their
  Organizations. San Francisco: Jossey-Bass, 1993.
Miller, J. G. Living Systems. New York: McGraw-Hill, 1978.
Mitroff, I. I., and Linstone, H. A. The Unbounded Mind: Breaking the Chains of Traditional Business
  Thinking. New York: Oxford University Press, 1993.
Myers, D. G. Psychology. (3rd ed.) New York: Worth, 1992.
Quinn, R. E., and Cameron, K. "Organizational Life Cycles and Shifting Criteria for Effectiveness:
  Some Preliminary Evidence." Management Science, 1983, 29 (1), 35–51.
Senge, P. M. The Fifth Discipline: The Art and Practice of the Learning Organization. New York: Double-
  day, 1990.

Vaill, P. B. *Managing as a Performing Art: New Ideas for a World of Chaotic Change.* San Francisco: Jossey-Bass, 1989.

Waddington, C. H. *The Man-Made Future.* New York: St. Martin's Press, 1978.

Wilson, I. "The State of Strategic Planning: What Went Wrong? What Goes Right?" Issues Paper no. 3. *Technological Forecasting and Social Change,* 1990, 37, 103–110.

Ziegenfuss, J. T., Jr. *Designing Organizational Futures.* Springfield, Ill.: Thomas, 1989.

ALBERT L. LORENZO is president of Macomb Community College, with district offices in Warren, Michigan, and chair of the National Consortium on Institutional Effectiveness and Student Success. He received the 1993 Management Recognition Award from the National Council for Research and Planning.

The system of quality-focused management (QFM) is presented, followed by an explanation of the departure it makes from established community college management practices. The utility of QFM for faculty, staff, and administrators is described.

Quality-Focused Management

Robbie Lee Needham

Managing for quality has many names: strategic quality management (SQM), continuous quality improvement (CQI), *Kaizen*, service quality (SQ), and total quality management (TQM). Regardless of the label, quality-focused management (QFM) is a management system—a philosophy, a set of tools, and a portfolio of organizational models.

The basic principles of this management system have been articulated by its originators (Deming, 1986; Juran, 1989; Crosby, 1985). Advocated by management professors, consultants, and practitioners, these principles are increasingly familiar to managers in the public and private sectors. Exposure to them has been so heavy in recent years that administrators are beginning to look beyond the basic concepts to long-term implications for management.

QFM Is a Management System

The following discussion describes the philosophy, tools, and management roles inherent to quality-focused management.

Philosophy. The foundations of QFM are customer satisfaction, continuous improvement of quality, and constancy of purpose, which is defining the business of an organization and concentrating on it. The customer, internal or external, defines quality for the provider, whose job it is to meet or exceed the customers' needs or expectations. Continuous improvement is the mental attitude that sustains individuals and organizations in the quest for quality.

The practices that enable institutions to implement QFM are process improvement, human resource development, and the use of the scientific method. Focusing on facts rather than intuition encourages staff to separate process problems from random errors made by individuals. Random errors are responsible for only 15 percent of the poor performance of organizations; process problems account for the rest. Thus, QFM directs the focus of improvement efforts to root causes within processes. Process improvement enables an institution to be more productive, often without increasing its work force.

The structures that drive QFM are quality teams, usually five to eight people, who focus on improving a process such as registration, purchasing, ordering textbooks, or student tracking. The people on the teams are selected from the process "owners"—those who work in the process and who supervise it, its suppliers, and its customers. Quality teams may be ad hoc, with a one-time goal, or standing, with ongoing responsibility.

Tools. Process improvement teams use the tools of QFM to identify and understand root causes of process problems as well as to collect and display information that directs their decisions. The standard tools for identifying a problem include brainstorming, nominal group technique, checksheet, and flowchart. For analyzing a problem there are tools such as the histogram, scatter diagram, control chart, and force field analysis. Additional tools can be used to identify and analyze problems: pareto chart, run chart, and cause and effect (fishbone) diagram (Brassard, 1991). Training in team building, conflict management, and group communications enables groups to use these technical tools. The tools are not difficult to learn and use; the people processes are the bigger challenge.

According to Harrington (1991), the work of process improvement teams usually results in streamlining operations by reducing or eliminating steps in the process that do not add value. Rework (correction of errors in document completion), repetition (transfer of a telephone call several times), waste (more photocopies than needed), breakdowns (incomplete distribution of information), and unnecessary complexity (multiple signatures of approval on a document) are some of the more common problems that make processes inefficient. Registration is a good example of a process in community colleges that can be improved through the work of teams. Consider the lines, excess paperwork, staff to process paperwork, repetition of tasks, and rework to correct errors. In what way(s) can registration be streamlined by reducing or eliminating steps that slow the process, create paperwork, or require staff attention?

Team members expect that the improvements that prove effective will be implemented. They also expect to keep monitoring the process to ensure that it remains within the improved parameters and to be alert to new opportunities for improvement. Teams need structure, resources, training, and coaching. Usually a steering committee, led by senior management, designates the teams, charters them, defines goals, and sets boundaries. The steering committee provides resources needed by the teams and removes barriers to their progress.

Management Roles. Under the QFM philosophy, roles and relationships change throughout the organization, perhaps most for managers, who become pilgrims on the journey of quality. They are vision givers and strategic thinkers and planners committed to meeting customer needs through continuous improvement. They manage processes rather than discrete tasks or functions and they orchestrate people-driven improvements. They are catalysts, coaches, team members, and teachers within the organization.

Departure from Current Practice

To say that QFM represents a departure from current management and governance practices in community colleges is an understatement. Quality-focused managers say that it is a dramatic change, one that requires a cultural change, a paradigm shift.

The established management paradigms are labeled "centralized," "authoritarian," "bureaucratic"; the emerging paradigms include the "high-performance work organization," the "commitment model," and the "learning organization." Some differences between these two approaches can be listed as follows:

Current Practice	Emerging Focus
Driven by the bottom line	Driven by the customer
Crisis management	Long-term commitment
Inversely related quality and costs	Directly related quality and costs
Quality can be assigned to one department.	Quality is built-in; it is everyone's job.

Management Orientation. All components of the emerging focus are departures, in varying degrees, from established community college management perspectives and practices. A significant departure is the focus on customers and their central role in defining quality in programs and services. It is difficult for some instructors and staff to acknowledge that programs and services have customers who know a lot about quality. Having thought that other people's opinions about quality really do not matter, staff must change perspectives to see "outsiders"—students, legislators, citizens, and employers—as customers and believe that their opinions about quality matter (Seymour, 1992).

The next challenge is even more difficult: identify internal and external customers, research their needs and expectations for quality, then set customer satisfaction as the standard for quality. Identifying customers and their expectations is not so intimidating as is accepting that the customer's definition of quality is paramount.

Having traditionally defined quality in terms of the resources applied to education, staff will find it a real change to define quality in terms of the use and results of resources. The results deemed important vary from college to college. They can include factors such as evidence of student learning and development, student goal achievement, student satisfaction with the college experience, employer satisfaction with graduates, transfer success of students, staff satisfaction with work, and the public image of the college.

Accustomed to defining quality through periodic inspections such as program review or accreditation, community colleges now must define quality as the results of individual and collective work, subject to continuous improvement. Colleges that choose this departure are freed from minimum standards of quality to set their own criteria. Further, they keep quality on the front burner, getting attention every day in every program. Choosing QFM thus enables colleges to be engaged in self-study daily, preparing for external review, so that it is not a monumental event occurring every so often.

Another real departure for community college management is relating the costs of education to quality (the costs of doing things right) or nonquality (the cost of doing things wrong). Fox Valley Technical College in Wisconsin has analyzed the costs of quality and has learned that costs and quality are directly related and that quality costs less than nonquality. In 1987–88 the college found that the cost of supporting the quality improvement thrust was $172,059, while the costs of nonconformance was $8,124,270 (Spanbauer, 1992).

The bottom-line and crisis management focus characteristic of many community colleges diverts management attention from the organization's long-term vitality. A transition to the long-term view of the emerging models is fundamental to improving quality. Quality, like perfection, is an elusive goal. Improvement is a continuous process, one that is supported by decisions to improve processes rather than fix problems, to find a solution to the root cause of a problem. Community college administrators often describe this change of perspective from short-term to long-term and the shift from fixing problems to improving processes as a departure, sometimes a rupture, from their established ways of doing things.

Current Practice	Emerging Focus
Who made the error?	What allowed the error to occur?
Employees are the problem.	Processes or systems are the problem.
Measure and change individuals.	Measure and change the processes.
Emphasis on tasks within functional units	Emphasis on processes across functional units

Manage Processes. Current management perspectives focus on people, especially when looking for errors or solving problems. Statisticians, including Deming, have demonstrated that people are responsible for only 15 per-cent of the errors that occur in a work process. Thus, the results of individual efforts—the services delivered to customers—are controlled by processes. It is a real departure from established practice in community college management to attend to processes rather than manage discrete tasks or separate organizational units.

In the new paradigm, managers learn first to understand work as processes, then to identify the major college processes and their managers, missions, and customers, both internal and external. Managers become responsible for understanding processes by flowcharting them, then for managing them so that each step adds value, variation is reduced, and staff working within the processes are encouraged to improve them continually. This is an ongoing effort since processes, left to themselves, tend to deteriorate and adapt continually for comfort, not efficiency.

Attending to processes usually results in management realizing that major processes cut across organizational boundaries. To manage them, managers must become a team, facilitating connections of staff across units. This, too, is a departure for many in community college management.

Current Practice	Emerging Focus
Understanding my job	Knowing how my job fits into the total process
Doing my job	Helping get things done
Individual effort	Teamwork

Teamwork. For QFM to work, managers must become committed to collaborative work throughout the institution. Collaboration does not mean more committees; rather, it means developing departments and service units into teams that become self-directed. For many administrators, giving up control is an unsettling departure from current practice. However, empowering others, allowing them to control their work, is the only way to get staff to work together for continuous improvement as a way of life (Byham, 1988). Sharing authority for decision making can be accomplished systematically and smoothly as managers and team members learn new roles.

Ongoing quality teams progress through four developmental stages. Each stage requires managers to be involved differently. In the form stage, managers are directive, presenting the institutional mission and goals and setting boundaries. In the storm phase, managers are delegative, helping team members fill team roles. Team members develop their own "rules" and procedures in the norm stage. Managers are in the room, but not at the team table. Moving to the perform stage, teams become self-directed work groups that are fully empowered, working toward college goals and objectives without supervision but with management support.

Community college teams, within departments and across functions, can become self-managing teams. So long as team membership remains stable, support is needed from management only in providing resources and removing barriers. Any time membership on the team changes, the team returns to stage one of its development and must work through each of the stages to become self-managing.

Current Practice	Emerging Focus
Staff	People
Control staff; motivate them.	Remove barriers; develop people.
You cannot trust anyone.	We are all in this together.

Perceptions of Staff. Current management models in community colleges isolate staff, build barriers, drive out trust, rob staff of satisfaction in their work, and respect the thinking of only a few. The emerging models respect each individual and stress organizing to utilize people in the institution fully. These models are designed to drive out fear, build trust, and emphasize that people want to act responsibly, do a good job, and feel good about their workplace.

The emerging models present three departures from current practice in community college management. The first departure involves the personnel function of the college. In addition to making sure that selection processes result in hiring the best person for the job, the personnel function in an institution involved with QFM ensures that orientation to the college and specific positions adequately prepares individuals to be successful on the job. Personnel evaluation systems and practices are reviewed and adjusted as necessary to support the focus on quality and the use of teams throughout the college. The personnel function also assists in recognizing and rewarding quality improvements.

Another departure is a new focus on staff development. Programs require redesign to support the development of quality-related skills. Resources for staff development are increased to 4 to 6 percent of the personnel budgets in the new models and may be redistributed, with staff receiving more than they have traditionally.

The third departure is in the organizational structure of the college. Most established community college structures come from two different models: the machine bureaucracy for support units and the professional bureaucracy for instruction (Mintzberg, 1983). The former separates functional units and manages them vertically, often with very close supervision. The latter is a more horizontal structure, separated into departments and disciplines, with faculty having considerable freedom to carry out their responsibilities.

The emerging management models represent a departure for community college management in both patterns. Management will become more horizontal, in practice if not in structure. The most significant departure will be in the management of support units, where decisions about quality and process improvement will be pushed low in the organization, thus decentralizing decisions about the ways in which goals and objectives are approached and work is accomplished. Many of the decisions will be made by self-directed cross-functional teams. These changes will require different management roles, attitudes, and behaviors to develop among leaders in order to empower staff who in the past have been told what to do, how to do it, and when it must be done.

In the instructional departments, management for quality will require change too. Identifying and managing instructional processes, as well as developing teams, many of which will be cross-disciplinary and become self-directed, will require a new kind of leadership and support from instructional administrators. With encouragement and support from administrators, faculty members will do more than teach. They will scan external markets, survey employers, conduct follow-up research with students, and assess customer needs—all in the name of improving quality. The instructional department of tomorrow will be a self-directed work team performing strategic management functions similar to those performed by senior administrators.

Using teams, respecting internal customers and suppliers, and engaging in continuous process improvement will require community college managers to adopt a favorable attitude toward staff as "people in the organization." Xerox has acknowledged the importance of people processes in implementing quality-focused management through the cause-effect (fishbone) diagram presented in Figure 5.1.

"Five of the six bones on the fish relate to people, and of these five, senior management behavior is both central to changing the culture for quality, and one of the most challenging," according to Rene Ewing, quality consultant of Xerox Corporation, Northwest Area (Ewing, 1992).

Governance. Involving people throughout the institution productively and creatively in decisions about their work affects governance. Research shows that fewer people feel disenfranchised, ignored, or distrustful as they break out of bureaucratic paradigms and behaviors. Instructors and staff become energized and excited by working with team members; they experience increasing satisfaction with their jobs and with the college. Even committee meetings become more productive for their members when the tools for decision making and teamwork are brought into meetings. Indeed, the emerging QFM models help develop and nurture participatory management as well as a win-win attitude throughout the college.

Figure 5.1. Supporting Elements for Transforming Xerox Corporation to a Quality Culture

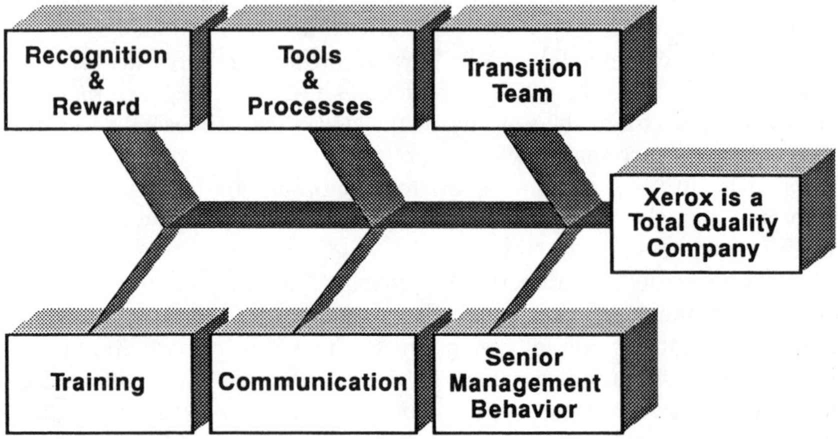

With QFM requiring such a departure from current management practices, what does it offer community colleges that makes it worth the effort?

Instructors. To instructors QFM offers a systematic approach to improving student success. It provides a set of easy-to-use research tools, the inducement to identify and manage classroom systems, and the requirement to be student-customer centered.

For example, QFM is being used to manage a program in Tacoma Community College, Washington, by teachers who seek to be student-centered in ways that improve retention and completion. These teachers now serve "customers" rather than students. They establish parameters for performance, structure experiences, and relate with customers in ways to empower them. They use information to monitor the effects of instructional strategies and change them continually. These instructors ask, "What can we do to help you learn?" They listen. Beyond the classroom, the teachers see themselves as customers (receiving students) and suppliers (sending customers to other courses, employers, communities, families). They seek feedback from the recipients of their students (that is, employers, communities, and so on) that will help them improve the program. In managing and assessing their processes, working in teams, and demonstrating concern about customer satisfaction, these teachers try to be positive role models for their student-customers and other teachers in the college (Lockemy and Summers, 1992). Instructors have as much to gain from QFM as administrators. They have as dramatic a paradigm shift to make as well.

Staff. For staff, who have traditionally been managed more like employees in industry, QFM provides an opportunity for increased involvement in decisions that affect their work. It offers opportunities to increase productivity, demonstrate responsibility, act with initiative, think creatively, and make decisions as individuals and team members. It results in empowerment (Block, 1987). In addition, QFM promotes increased interaction with colleagues throughout the college, without the artificial barriers erected by vertical management hierarchies and the label "nonprofessional." It offers increased job satisfaction. Further, QFM makes it possible for staff to identify more deeply and personally with the college's mission and goals.

Administrators. For administrators, QFM provides new ways and different structures for operating institutions (Spanbauer, 1992). It helps administrators manage systematically, for institutional effectiveness. Adopting customer satisfaction as a standard for quality ensures that community colleges will do the right things to remain vital over the long haul. Managing to improve processes ensures that colleges will do things right while making the best use of resources.

Managing for quality guides administrators toward vital, more relevant and flexible standards for evaluation and accountability. Thus, QFM pushes colleges beyond minimum standards and external requirements for quality to internal commitments that are monitored daily and improved continuously.

Quality-focused management also supplies structures and tools to decentralize decision making and problem solving, develop and empower staff, eliminate bureaucracy, improve productivity, as well as increase morale and job satisfaction. It aids administrators in making community colleges more flexible organizations while simultaneously preventing them from being trapped in the status quo. While administrators are responsible for seeing that all major systems are managed for the benefit of customers, they are freed from crisis management. Executive administrators devote more time to leadership—knowing the external environment, thinking about the future, and visioning.

The QFM system clarifies administrative responsibilities at all levels of the institution. It helps administrators make better, data-driven decisions, and it requires that they seek root causes of problems as well as consider the long-term implications of decisions. It also helps administrators focus on the most important management responsibilities and respect people throughout the college. It offers structures and practices for making hard choices: doing more with less or restructuring the college. Finally, QFM gives administrators a philosophy and system that can take current organizations to a new level of fitness, one at which community colleges can become learning organizations, continually expanding their capacity to create their futures. After all, "Through learning we re-create ourselves" (Senge, 1990, p. 14).

References

Block, P. *The Empowered Manager: Positive Political Skills at Work*. San Francisco: Jossey-Bass, 1987.

Brassard, M. *Memory Jogger Plus*. Methuen, MA: GOAL/QPC, 1991.

Byham, W. C. *Zapp! The Lightning of Empowerment*. New York: Fawcett Columbine, 1988.

Crosby, P. B. *Quality Without Tears*. New York: McGraw-Hill, 1985.

Deming, W. E. *Out of the Crisis*. Cambridge, MA: MIT Center for Advanced Engineering Study, 1986.

Ewing, R. "Quest for Quality." Training seminar presented at Tacoma Community College, Tacoma, Wash., Oct. 1992.

Harrington, H. J. *Business Process Improvement: The Breakthrough Strategy for Total Quality, Productivity, and Competitiveness*. New York: McGraw-Hill, 1991.

Juran, J. M. *Juran on Leadership for Quality: An Executive Handbook*. New York: Free Press, 1989.

Lockemy, M. J. and Summers, S. "Our Journey." Paper presented at Tacoma Community College, Tacoma, Wash., Dec. 1992.

Mintzberg, H. *Structure in Fives: Designing Effective Organizations*. New York: Prentice Hall, 1983.

Senge, P. *Fifth Discipline*. New York: Doubleday, 1990.

Seymour, D. T. *On Q: Causing Quality in Higher Education*. New York: Macmillan and American Council on Education, 1992.

Spanbauer, S. J. *A Quality System for Education*. Milwaukee: Quality Press, American Society for Quality Control, 1992.

ROBBIE LEE NEEDHAM *is executive director of ADVANCE SMF, Inc., in Tacoma, Washington, a consulting firm that focuses on planning, evaluation, and management for quality.*

Colleges that put students first are concerned with what students learn and how they are treated. Students who are educated in such an environment receive the added benefit of exposure to quality management and customer-oriented organizational culture. Ultimately, student satisfaction affects retention and future enrollment growth.

Students First! Reconceptualizing Support Services

James L. Hudgins, Sandi Oliver, Starnell K. Williams

When any organization seeks to optimize its effectiveness, it must consider the recipient of its service or product for ultimate evidence of success or failure. Colleges, like any structured organization, evaluate themselves based on the outcomes that are produced and the processes by which those outcomes are achieved. Specifically, colleges that place a high value on services designed to enhance student success and satisfaction are best able to demonstrate their own institutional effectiveness.

In recent years a great deal has been written about the need for educational accountability. In the beginning of the institutional effectiveness movement, relatively few colleges were thinking in terms of how they could phrase and answer questions about the value and quality of the institution and the satisfaction of students. Today, if a college has not already made a commitment to the philosophy of accountability and consequent student success, it must certainly feel nervous about its future.

Perhaps the most essential benchmark a college must establish is a good definition of what its business is, what product it produces, and who its customers are. Successful institutions have come to believe they are in the business of providing a quality learning environment, that their product is excellent education and support services, and that their customers are the students and potential students they serve.

As elemental as it seems, this trilogy was not always accepted as fact. Formerly, institutions appeared to think students were their products, not their clients. Along with the evolution of a customer-centered orientation in the early to mid-1980s coupled with the strengthening of the institutional effectiveness movement, one simple truth has emerged: colleges are successful when their students are successful.

NEW DIRECTIONS FOR COMMUNITY COLLEGES, no. 84, Winter 1993 © Jossey-Bass Publishers

This statement reflects an institutional culture that values service to students second to no other purpose or function. When colleges dedicate the full scope of their resources and tailor planning to identify and meet the needs of the student-customer, effectiveness, accountability, and success will follow. Leaders need to determine what is required for each student to be successful at their college and how to serve students effectively.

Over the past decade, the assessment of student success has moved from an experimental practice at a few institutions to a national requirement. More than forty states have educational accountability mandates, and all six regional accrediting associations have incorporated the measurement of student learning outcomes into their accreditation criteria.

For much of their history, colleges expressed quality in terms of faculty credentials, physical facilities, learning resources, and degrees awarded. The accountability movement has encouraged higher education to think about quality and effectiveness in different terms—student learning. Edgerton (1990) describes assessment as "a mindset that asks questions—good questions, hard questions, legitimate questions—about what and how much students are learning" (p. 5).

Operationalizing Institutional Effectiveness

At Midlands Technical College (MTC) in Columbia, South Carolina, an institutional effectiveness program was initiated in 1987 in conjunction with reaffirmation of accreditation with the Southern Association of Colleges and Schools—the first accrediting body to emphasize student learning assessment as a condition of accreditation. For MTC, establishing processes for ongoing self-evaluation became as important as measuring outcomes.

The first step toward verifiable effectiveness was to ask and answer three basic questions: What is the mission (business) of the college? What are the major results expected from the achievement of the mission? What specific evidence are we willing to accept that these results have been achieved?

As part of the comprehensive strategic planning process that followed, the college rewrote its mission statement and identified its core values. The first of the four MTC value statements reads "Commitment to Students: Belief in the priority of providing the finest instruction, resources and support services to enhance the growth and development of our students."

To help the college community understand the comprehensive nature of institutional effectiveness, the college adopted and communicated a diagram of institutional effectiveness developed by the National Alliance of Community and Technical Colleges (see Figure 6.1).

The next critical step involved identifying the characteristics of an effective community college and specifying the characteristics most appropriate for

Figure 6.1. Model of Institutional Effectiveness

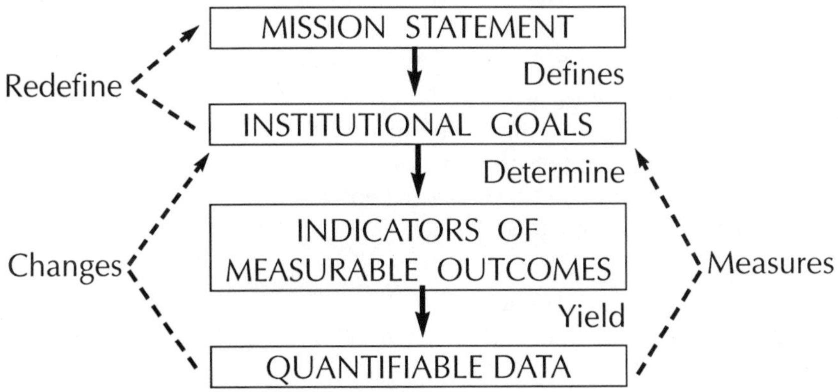

```
                    ┌──────────────────────────────┐
              ↗     │    MISSION  STATEMENT         │
  Redefine ◀       └──────────────┬───────────────┘ Defines
            ↖                     ▼
              ↖   ┌──────────────────────────────┐
                  │  INSTITUTIONAL  GOALS         │
                  └──────────────┬───────────────┘
             ↗                    ▼  Determine  ↖
           ↗       ┌──────────────────────────────┐  ↖
  Changes◀        │      INDICATORS  OF           │   ↖ Measures
           ↖      │  MEASURABLE  OUTCOMES         │   ↗
             ↖    └──────────────┬───────────────┘  ↗
               ↖                  ▼  Yield        ↗
                 ↖ ┌──────────────────────────────┐↗
                   │    QUANTIFIABLE DATA          │
                   └──────────────────────────────┘
```

Source: National Alliance of Community and Technical Colleges.

MTC in view of its mission. Ewell and Lisensky (1988) of the National Center for Higher Education Management Systems (NCHEMS) identify three characteristics of effective colleges: they clearly state the kinds of outcomes they are trying to produce, they explicitly assess the degree to which they are attaining those outcomes, and they make appropriate changes to improve the situation where the data warrants.

Three characteristics that differentiate high-performing colleges from mediocre ones have been identified: reputation for quality, distinctiveness, and innovation; flexible strategies for delivering programs and services; and systems for evaluating and improving performance (Alfred and others, 1992).

Effective community colleges define quality and attempt to measure it. Midlands Technical College sought to define and measure quality through a process known as critical success factors developed by the Sloan School of Business at MIT. The process argues that everything a business does is not equally important to the success of the business. If the business identifies, promotes, and measures those critical functions, it will succeed. The logic also applies to educational institutions.

Through a modified Delphi process, MTC identified six factors critical to the success of the college: accessible, comprehensive programs of high quality; student satisfaction and retention; posteducation satisfaction and success; economic development and community involvement; sound, effective resource management; and dynamic organizational involvement and development.

Under the six factors critical to success, the college identified twenty indicators of effectiveness. Figure 6.2 details the critical success factors and institutional effectiveness indicators. Two of the factors and seven of the indicators relate directly to student success:

Student Satisfaction and Retention
Accurate entry testing and course placement
Retention to achievement of student goals
Satisfaction with instruction and personal growth
Assessment of student services

Posteducation Satisfaction and Success
Graduate employment and continuing education
Employer satisfaction with graduates
Alumni satisfaction with education

After determining the performance criteria most essential to the success of the college, an implementation plan was developed. To implement an assessment program successfully, essential support systems must be in place. Such systems include enlisting the president and board of trustees' support, linking assessment to the college's mission, involving all units of the college, establishing an organizational structure to manage and monitor institutional effectiveness, determining how to pay for assessment activities, demonstrating that assessment data are used in decision making, and developing essential partnerships.

Perhaps the most essential element of a successful college-wide assessment program is leadership—from the president, executive staff, and faculty leaders.

Charles J. McClain, commissioner of the Missouri Coordinating Board of Higher Education, observes, "The difference between those institutions that are simply going through the motions of a compliance mode of quasi-action and those that have made a true commitment to institutional change through assessment is quite simple—leadership" (1991, p. 5).

Partnerships are both internal and external. No single unit of the college, be it faculty or president, can unilaterally lead the successful implementation of an institution-wide assessment program. Partnerships between student development services, academic affairs, fiscal affairs, and the president's office must be developed.

External partnerships are equally important. The advice, consultation, and expertise of external partners are essential. Some of these partners include regional accrediting bodies and the National Consortium for Institutional Effectiveness and Student Success in the Community College.

Figure 6.2. Midlands Technical College Critical Success Factors
and Institutional Effectiveness Indicators

-A- Accessible, Comprehensive Programs of High Quality	A-1 Access and Equity	A-2 Achievement in General Education	A-3 Assessment of the Academic Major	A-4 Successful Articulation/ Transfer
-B- Student Satisfaction and Retention	B-1 Accurate Entry Testing and Course Placement	B-2 Retention to Achievement of Student Goals	B-3 Satisfaction with Instruction and Personal Growth	B-4 Assessment of Student Services
-C- Post Education Satisfaction and Success	C-1 Graduate Employment/ Continuing Education	C-2 Employer Satisfaction with Graduates	C-3 Alumni Satisfaction with Education/ Training	
-D- Economic Development and Community Involvement	D-1 Education in Support of Economic Development	D-2 Positive Community/ College Interaction	D-3 Alumni Support and Involvement	
-E- Sound, Effective Resource Management	E-1 Acquisition of Public/Private Resources	E-2 Facility Adequacy, Use and Condition	E-3 Distribution of Resources	
-F- Dynamic Organizational Involvement and Development	F-1 Ongoing Professional Development of Commission, Faculty and Staff	F-2 Affirmative Action Plan	F-3 Support for Equity in Employee Salary/Benefits	

As MTC introduced an institutional effectiveness process and incorporated its philosophy into routine functions, it also experienced a cultural change. With the focus of all college processes shifted to student success, the entire college joined in discovering ways to make routine functions and procedures easier for students and more hassle-free.

The registration process has traditionally been a frustrating experience for college students. So it was this aspect of initial contact that was the first to receive special attention at MTC. The college formed a cross-functional registration committee unlike any other group that had previously studied entry services. With the single mandate of simplifying the process and making registration pleasant for students, this innovative group tackled problems ranging from long lines to the need for additional data entry terminals and quick-fix problem areas. Very quickly registration changed dramatically to become relatively stress-free for students and staff alike.

Evidence of a student-friendly culture is exemplified by MTC's desire to seek input from its students. "How's It Going?" posters appeared all over the campuses. These updated suggestion boxes were designed to be a direct pipeline to the president's ear. Students, faculty, and staff quickly learned to use the poster's reply cards to praise a program or service and offer suggestions for continuous improvement in almost all areas of the college.

A good example of the college's desire to gather suggestions from its customers is the annual meeting of senior college administration with the members of the college's Ambassador Assembly. Competing for the privilege of serving the college, ambassadors are students selected on the basis of their grades and demographics to represent the college in the community. In the annual workshops the ambassadors are asked two questions: What does MTC do well? What can MTC do better? Of significance is the fact that the ambassador suggestions were incorporated into the college's strategic planning process. As a result of their input, concrete changes were made, including alterations in campus lighting and security, bookstore policies, and packaging of courses to better fit the schedules of working students.

Emphasis on Student Success

The shift in focus to a student orientation through assessment of student needs and institutional planning to meet those needs has resulted in the pursuit of alternative models for student entry and enrollment services, and counseling and curriculum development. Six practical questions must be answered when establishing student assessment programs: What issues need to be addressed? What information will be collected? How and when will the information be collected? How will findings be communicated? How will the results be used for improvement? What resources are required? Addressing each of these areas individually reveals many of the major points to consider in an effective student assessment program.

What Issues Need to Be Addressed? One of the most important questions a college can ask itself concerns what information is being obtained by entry testing and exit exams. It is grossly unfair to ask students to perform tasks for which they are not prepared at entry. The data collected at entry should be used to place students in environments that will be most conducive to their success. This assessment may include placement into developmental studies areas for students who are not yet ready to attempt college-level work. These so-called at-risk students may include single parents, homemakers, reentry adults, minorities, students with disabilities, entering students, students with high financial need, academically underprepared students, and students with no clear direction. Early evaluation can help a college determine how best to meet the special needs of these groups.

What Information Will Be Collected? If students are asked to state their intended goal when they enter college, it becomes possible to measure goal fulfillment at exit. Commonly accepted student success indicators measure the retention or persistence of entering students. For the college-wide population, factors impacting retention include more accurate placement and advisement for entering students; preenrollment "Student Orientation for Success" sessions for students assessed to be at risk; linkage to support service areas based on identified student needs; increased emphasis on customer service, quality services, instructional quality, and educational performance; and changes in enrollment processes. For academically underprepared students, the following indicators impact retention: curriculum restructuring in developmental studies (DVS), changes in instructional delivery (self-paced to lectures or labs), changes in the DVS grading system, improved linkages between DVS and curriculum courses, and better placement of students into DVS courses via assessment and advisement. The retention of minority students may be affected by the college's commitment to access and equity; an increased focus on customer service, student success in the classroom, and faculty and staff sensitivity to cultural diversity; student support functions (e.g., African-American Student Organization, study groups, support personnel) and better orientation and increased communications that link student needs to support areas.

Assessment of basic skills and general education competencies are necessary to any holistic evaluation of student success. Especially compelling is the need for the college to measure student competencies in their major field of study. Collecting information about student satisfaction with the college can be extremely revealing (see Table 6.1). Assessment of a student's personal growth and development is, of course, subjective but can also be of value (see Table 6.2). The institution should examine the success rate of its transfer students and determine what factors contribute to their success or failure at senior institutions. The transferability of curricula designed for transfer should be verified and evaluated. Colleges should also ask employers how they value the education and job performance of the college's graduates. Students' employment success in their major field should also be monitored.

Table 6.1. Student Satisfaction with College

	Midlands Technical College	National
I am proud of my accomplishments at college.	4.67	4.25
The college helped me meet goals I came to achieve.	4.57	4.09
I would recommend the college to others.	4.56	4.13
If choosing a college again, I would choose this one.	4.31	3.88
The college welcomes and uses student feedback.	3.99	3.62

Note: Five-point scale.

Source: Midlands Technical College, College Outcomes Survey, Spring 1992.

Table 6.2. Students' Self-Perceived Personal Growth

Midlands Technical College Items Indicating Highest Growth	Midlands Technical College	National
Setting life direction	2.62	2.52
Becoming academically competent	2.58	2.42
Developing self-confidence	2.55	2.41
Increasing intellectual curiosity	2.52	2.44
Implementing long-term life goals	2.52	2.41
Improving ability to relate to others	2.45	2.36
Taking responsibility for own behavior	2.45	2.41
Increasing self-understanding	2.45	2.35
Making a lifelong commitment to learning	2.41	2.35

Note: Three-point scale.

Source: Midlands Technical College, College Outcomes Survey, Spring 1992.

Because Midlands Technical College places heavy emphasis on career education leading to productive employment in the college's service region, special attention is given to assessment of technical and vocational programs. One of the most comprehensive strategies for ensuring that students are exposed to a relevant, quality learning environment is the academic program review process for all associate degree programs. The following data elements are included in an academic program review: achievement of goals; program GPA; mastery of capstone competencies; mastery of general education core; program statistics including enrollment, cost, retention rate, and number of graduates; employment success; surveys of students, alumni, employers, and lay advisory committees.

Midlands Technical College is sensitive to practical workplace skills employers expect and require of technical/community college graduates. In many areas, the DACUM (Developing A CUrriculuM) process is used as part of a program review involving members of the business community in establishing a set of expectations and capstone competencies for each academic area. The program faculty rely on the DACUM's input when determining course content, methods of information delivery, and mechanisms for assessing capstone competencies. In all cases, program faculty work with education division administrators to develop appropriate standards. Various measures of accountability are built into the process.

Another important assessment strategy for measuring student progress is longitudinal tracking of mathematical and language skills through a series of courses presented in a structured sequence. Sequenced course objectives allow the MTC tracking system to identify strengths and weaknesses in the curriculum. Tracking data used in concert with classroom research is used to modify and improve curricula. Recent results in the college's English department involving a thousand students resulted in a course design that allowed students' writing abilities to evolve from their readings. A parallel result in the math department led to course objectives becoming more clearly defined and correlated. Tracking students' progression through course sequences resulted in increased faculty expectations and adjustments in the course content to enhance student success in meeting those expectations.

How and When Will Information Be Collected? Colleges should collect information about their students throughout the educational process. Educational plans developed at entry can be periodically updated and evaluated at exit. Follow-up information is essential to knowing how graduates' experiences at the colleges affected their lives. A model of data collection points is presented in Table 6.3.

How Will Findings Be Communicated? Using the organizational structure of the college, student services personnel can disseminate information through written reports, newsletters, and open forums for the college's staff and faculty. By maintaining open communication with the faculty, these personnel can share information that will affect the design of curricula and the selection of teaching methodology. Departmental and task force meetings should often revisit the topic of student assessment and connect data collection with techniques implemented in the classroom.

How Will Results Be Used? By the use of person-interaction modeling, predictions can be made about behavior that will result when certain types of individuals interact with certain types of environments. The college can combine challenges and support to produce developmental dissonance and growth for its students. The campus environment must reflect a comprehensive desire to provide programs and services that aid student development.

Table 6.3. Midlands Technical College Data Collection Points

At Entry	Participation	At Exit	Follow-up
Educational plans	Enrollment	Exit Skills	Transfer data
Student	patterns	CAAP	Enrollment
background	Academic	Discipline exams	Performance
Student needs	performance	Academic	Employment
Test scores	Services used	performance	information
ASSET	Satisfaction/involve-	GPA	Job data
ACT	ment information	Course grades	Student
SAT	Student surveys	Student opinions	perceptions
Discipline based	Focus groups	and plans	Employer
Perceptions of	Interviews	Surveys	perceptions
college		Interviews	Licensure tests
Entering stu-		Focus groups	Student opinions
dent survey			and plans
			Alumni surveys

What Resources Are Required? The expense of student assessment can be expressed by the equation Expenses – Benefits = Costs. In other words, the institution must decide whether the resources required to determine student needs are worth the potential benefit to the student. This is the same as trying to decide whether it is better to operate blindly or to concentrate on providing the precise service needed to be effective.

Expenses include the cost of assessment instruments and associated scoring charges, administrative costs, and any additional support personnel required. The benefits to be expected include service/program achievements, image enhancement, and higher student success rates. Also of benefit are increases in revenue that may be realized by greater student retention, higher new student enrollment, and potential new grant funds and contributions to scholarships.

Midlands Technical College has developed a nationally recognized, comprehensive model of student success that integrates planning and evaluation to foster student goal achievement and institutional development.

The MTC Assessment Model

Midlands Technical College's approach to student success focuses on how the college can effectively develop an educational environment conducive to the positive achievements of diverse student populations. Recognizing that all students do not respond to an educational environment in the same way, the college employs a person-environment model to assess student goals, backgrounds, needs, satisfaction, achievement, and personal growth (see Figure 6.3). A student cohort tracking system is used to monitor and analyze patterns of student subpopulations by a number of variables. These data are combined with information obtained from student surveys, testing, interviews, and focus groups collected at key points in the student's matriculation through and beyond the college. Faculty, staff, and students review these findings and formulate recommendations for improvements throughout the college's planning and evaluation system to modify the college environment and enhance positive student outcomes.

Since Midlands Technical College began student success monitoring in 1989, initiatives have included developing student educational plans at entry, including information on student goals, backgrounds, characteristics, and needs; integrated assessment, orientation, and advisement processes; Student Orientation for Success seminars for entering students; college success courses; an automated follow-up system on student needs; centralized advisement centers on each campus staffed by professionals; developmental academic advising separated from scheduling process; automated tools such as on-line advisor files and a degree audit system; college-wide training in customer service and sensitivity to diversity; updating student goals each term as part of registration; and modification to the registration process, including application deadlines.

Figure 6.3. The Midlands Technical College Assessment Plan

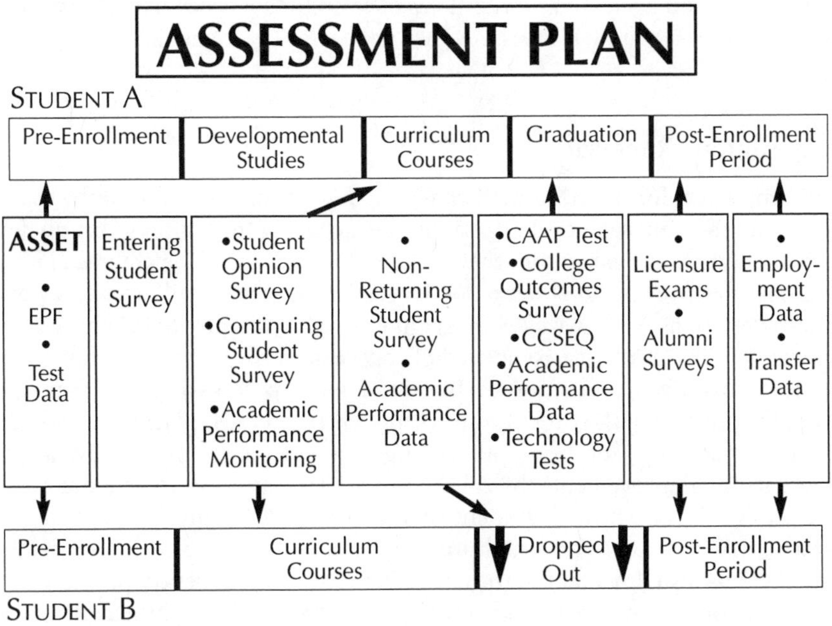

| ASSESSMENT PLAN |

STUDENT A

Pre-Enrollment	Developmental Studies	Curriculum Courses	Graduation	Post-Enrollment Period

| ASSET • EPF • Test Data | Entering Student Survey | •Student Opinion Survey •Continuing Student Survey •Academic Performance Monitoring | • Non-Returning Student Survey • Academic Performance Data | •CAAP Test •College Outcomes Survey •CCSEQ •Academic Performance Data •Technology Tests | Licensure Exams • Alumni Surveys | • Employment Data • Transfer Data |

Pre-Enrollment	Curriculum Courses	Dropped Out	Post-Enrollment Period

STUDENT B

Midlands Technical College has also made modifications in the environment to serve the needs of targeted at-risk populations. These changes have included restructuring the instructional diversity and grading systems of developmental studies courses to more closely resemble college-level courses; placing undecided students into a special major that allows exploration of academic programs and advisement by career counselors; including minority access and equity as a major college goal with special support groups, student organizations, peer mentoring, and orientation activities; and offering seminars and workshops for students with disabilities, single parents, homemakers, minorities, and other at-risk populations.

Since 1989, the college has experienced significant enrollment growth while maintaining a 90 percent student satisfaction rating in most areas. Overall retention of students toward their goals has increased 6.4 percent, with increases of 7 to 17 percent for at-risk student groups. In addition, more than 90 percent of graduates are employed or continuing their education within a year of graduation. More than 90 percent of sophomore-level students indicate the college has contributed to their personal growth in areas such as career direction and academic autonomy.

The MTC student success model was honored with a 1992 Pyramid Award presented by the American College Personnel Association, the National Council on Student Development, and the National Association of Student Personnel Administrators for outstanding achievement in student development in two-year colleges. Midlands Technical College also received a 1992 national retention award from Noel-Levitz. The college's student success model was featured in a 1993 national teleconference sponsored by American College Testing (ACT).

Continuous Renewal

It is important for the continued vitality of any program or philosophy that it be monitored and rejuvenated periodically. Recalling the warning that all data are of questionable value until they are used, colleges that have embraced institutional effectiveness and orientation for student success should reevaluate and modify systems and processes over time. As an example, MTC charged an Intake Review Task Force comprised of college personnel from cross-functional units to investigate and report on the entire intake process, including application for financial aid, student inquiry, the entry process, placement, advisement, scheduling, and book purchasing. The purpose of this review was to evaluate the improvements the college had made in an effort to be more accessible to students. Through student surveys and direct examination of all routine entry services, the resulting conclusion of the task force yielded suggestions for refinement in the college's recruitment and entry processes. By checking on systems that had been in place for several years, the college was able to make additional improvements on behalf of students. This is an example of continuous quality improvement and the good sense of asking students how they value the functions intended to be customer-oriented.

Student Success Equals Mission Accomplishment

Should colleges base effectiveness programs on student success? There remains one last compelling argument for an affirmative response. In financial circumstances that leave a college struggling to match dwindling resources to increasing needs, a commitment to evaluating effectiveness and student outcomes becomes essential. When tough choices must be made, a college that has defined areas critical to success and tied student outcomes to mission accomplishment can more easily reach consensus on prioritizing resources. When a college is confident the definition and delivery of its services is optimized for effectiveness, both the institution and its students are the winners.

References

Alfred, R., and others. Making Community Colleges More Effective. Ann Arbor, Mich.: Community College Consortium, 1992.

Edgerton, R. "Assessment at Halftime." Change, Oct. 1990, p. 5.

Ewell, P. T., and Lisensky, R. P. Assessing Institutional Effectiveness: Redirecting the Self-Study Process. Boulder, Colo.: Consortium for the Advancement of Private Higher Education, National Center for Higher Education Management Systems, 1988.

McClain, C. J. "Education with Integrity." AACJC Journal, Apr.–May 1991, p. 5.

JAMES L. HUDGINS is president of Midlands Technical College in Columbia, South Carolina. He serves on the board of directors of the American Association of Community Colleges and is vice chair of the National Consortium for Institutional Effectiveness and Student Success in the Community College.

SANDI OLIVER is associate vice president for student development services at Midlands Technical College.

STARNELL K. WILLIAMS is associate vice president for advancement at Midlands Technical College.

PART THREE

Challenges for Leadership

In order for our colleges and universities to benefit fully from the skills and talents of the diverse men and women who are increasingly entering the managerial ranks, we must substantially modify individual attitudes and behaviors and make radical changes in organizational structures. Are we up to it?

New Players in Management

Ruth Burgos-Sasscer

Last year a search committee at Harry S. Truman College, one of the City Colleges of Chicago, interviewed six finalists for a high-level administrative position. Two of the candidates were African American, one was Latino, one was Asian American, and two were Americans of Northern European descent. Four of these candidates were women. Since Truman College serves a multiethnic, multiracial urban community and has a strong affirmative action policy in place, the diversity of these finalists was not unusual. However, ending a search for an administrative position with such a diverse pool of candidates is not the rule on most college campuses.

Demographic changes in American society suggest that this phenomenon will be occurring with increasing frequency. The Hudson Institute report *Workforce 2000* predicted in 1987 that by the end of the century, only 15 percent of the new entrants to the work force will be white males, compared to 47 percent in 1985 (Jamieson and O'Mara, 1991). Indeed, new candidates for jobs already are increasingly female and increasingly people of color, and for the first time since World War I, a growing number are immigrants.

In addition to these demographic shifts, the U.S. Bureau of Labor Statistics predicts that between 1990 and 2000, annual growth in the U.S. work force will slow to 1.2 percent, down from the 2 percent growth during the previous decades. Thus, recruitment and integration of capable men and women from all backgrounds and all walks of life into the work force of our colleges are to be expected.

In light of this reality, executives are learning to manage an employee population that is increasingly diverse in terms of gender, race, age, ethnicity, disability, social class, and previous work experiences. College and university presidents, for example, are beginning to ask questions about the diverse members who are gradually joining their managerial ranks: How do they fare? Do they "fit in"? Are they becoming effective team members? Are they perceived as enriching the life of the institution or as having a divisive effect? Are their skills and knowledge recognized and valued? How significant is their contribution to the achievement of institutional goals? Managing diversity successfully may be as challenging as it is rewarding.

Managing Diversity Is Not Affirmative Action

Community college leaders are coming to realize that managing diversity is more than providing access to new groups. It is not a matter of numbers, although hiring qualified persons from a pool of candidates that reflect the demographics of the community being served is a first step. Managing diversity has to do with cultivating, strengthening, and utilizing the talents and skills of all employees so that individual and organizational goals are achieved. "The problem," says R. Roosevelt Thomas, Jr., executive director of the American Institute for Managing Diversity, "is not getting them [women and minorities] in at the entry level; the problem is making better use of their potential at every level, especially in middle-management and leadership positions" (Thomas, 1990, p. 108).

Managing diversity is as much a bottom-line issue as it is a matter of attitudes and behavior. James E. Preston, CEO of Avon Products, Inc., speaks for his peers when he states, "This is not some type of benevolent activity on our part. There is self-interest here" (Thomas, 1991, p. 164). In the corporate as well as in the academic work setting, the successful management of diverse employees is driven by concerns for global awareness, the quality revolution, and the competitive edge. A basic assumption is that the talents, skills, and perspectives that diverse individuals bring to the workplace are a key to meeting the challenges of the twenty-first century (Fernandez, 1991).

The New, Diverse Team Players

It is no doubt easier to manage a group of individuals who share the same values and beliefs and, in general, behave in a similar fashion than it is to manage a heterogeneous group. Nevertheless, for colleges to achieve goals it is important to manage qualified and talented individuals who are not the same and who do not necessarily aspire to be the same. The newcomers to college administration may hold the same academic degrees and perhaps have had similar professional experiences, but they may also dress, speak, think, and behave differently than each other and than those who have been in the system a long time.

In the past, "assimilation" made the task of management easier. White male–dominated corporations set the standards for behavior in the workplace, and managing was largely a matter of enforcing those standards and rewarding those who met them best. Those few individuals whose gender or ethnic values influenced their behavior in ways that went against the grain were often deemed less capable. This negative perception changed only if the noncon-formists were willing and able to put aside their differences and behave like the dominant group. As many immigrants know, the process of acculturation is often painful, even when it is considered desirable (Thomas, 1991).

Some still advocate a melting pot in which distinct ethnic identities are boiled down into one American puree, but given the changing demographics of our country, the shrinking work force, and the interdependence of nations, assimilation is no longer practical or, it can be argued, desirable. The most suc-cessful organizations of today and tomorrow are clearly those that capitalize on the varied skills, talents, insights, and views of their diverse employees (Kanter, 1989; Jamieson and O'Mara, 1991).

Radical Changes Are Needed

Experts agree that if the United States is to reap the benefits of its diverse pop-ulation, it must provide a work environment that recognizes that individuals are different and that diversity is an advantage if it is valued and cultivated rather than restricted (Jamieson and O'Mara, 1991). Creating such an envi-ronment in academic work settings is made difficult by a bureaucratic culture that rewards conformity and imposes a structure that penalizes openness to new ideas, flexibility, and cooperation. Union-management contracts and gov-ernment-mandated personnel laws have contributed to increased rights for workers but also to greater rigidity (Jamieson and O'Mara, 1991). Community colleges that want to capitalize on and nurture diversity in management will have to make radical changes in policies and practices, development programs, and organization structure, among others. Clearly, new management models and leadership styles will be needed.

The Corporate Model

Not surprisingly, some of these changes are already occurring in the business world. In response to competitive pressures, a new breed of executives is behaving noticeably differently than traditional bureaucrats. To begin with, they are disregarding the hierarchical distinctions of title, task, and department. Their focus is on the collective talents of members of the group rather than on the skills of one individual. They find that tasks are best accomplished by teams of individuals who have the skills to do the job, regardless of their back-grounds or titles (Kanter, 1989).

These corporate leaders seek and welcome diversity at all levels, but espe-cially at the management level, because they are aware that higher-quality solutions are found when a team of people views problems from different per-spectives, expertise, and styles (Jamieson and O'Mara, 1991; Gordon, 1992).

They concur with management guru Tom Peters that "the power of the team is so great that it is often wise to violate apparent common sense and force a team structure on almost anything" (Peters, 1987, p. 364).

Fortunately, corporate restructuring is taking place when women and minorities are entering the workplace in increasing numbers. The flexible approaches, group orientation, linguistic skills, and bicultural perspectives of these groups are precisely what corporate America needs to gain the competitive edge—and the most enlightened leaders know it.

Strategies for Change in Community Colleges

In community colleges, as in nonacademic work settings, the leadership of the chief executive officer is crucial to bringing about important changes. Thus, to make full use of the diverse skills of new managers, college presidents must articulate and communicate a clear vision of the goals they hope to achieve. These presidents must also have in place a plan of action that reflects a personal commitment to the proposed changes. Then, they must make it happen. It is in this spirit that the following strategies are recommended.

Insist on a diverse pool of qualified candidates for managerial positions; the pool should include women, ethnic and racial minorities, white males, and so forth.

Identify and meaningfully address any inequities in salaries of men, women, and minorities who hold similar managerial positions.

Adopt policies and procedures that minimize inherent unfairness to certain groups (for example, evaluation procedures based only on performance and as measured by criteria agreed on by both evaluators and evaluees).

Adopt flexible policies to address family needs (maternity, parental, and caregiver) and child care.

Disseminate information about demographics of students, faculty, and staff and report on the status of minorities on campus.

Present seminars and workshops on diversity issues, such as work style differences and differences in values, beliefs, and behavior.

Celebrate events that are part of other people's culture, such as national holidays and the birthdays of prominent persons.

Provide opportunities for social events that bring together diverse staff members and their families.

Set the example of behaving more as a colleague than as a boss (share information and power, mentor, coach, and delegate).

Provide training in cross-cultural communication so that managers can communicate more effectively with each other, and give constructive and critical feedback to subordinates.

Offer seminars and workshops on how affirmative action and equal employment opportunity programs work.

Encourage innovation by rewarding and implementing new ideas regardless of who offers them.

Minimize hierarchical structures by eliminating functional barriers (rigid job descriptions and lines of authority) and promoting the idea of managers as facilitators.

Get team members not to fear change, and even to love it, by encouraging openness to new ideas, trying new ways of performing tasks, and preparing for the unexpected.

Men and women with diverse backgrounds are increasingly entering the ranks of community college management. They are becoming members of decision-making teams that are responsible for developing and achieving vital institutional goals. Their diverse talents, skills, and perspectives are particularly welcome at a time when national leaders are clamoring for accessible and appropriate responses to fast-changing international, economic, and political demands.

Leaders are quickly learning that building teams with players who are unlike each other, and who do not necessarily want to be like each other, is not easy. Nevertheless, this task can be successfully accomplished if each leader becomes what Tom Peters says all leaders must become: a "lover of change and preacher of vision and shared values" (1985, p. 53).

References

Fernandez, J. Managing a Diverse Work Force. Lexington, Mass.: Lexington Books, 1991.

Gordon, J. "Rethinking Diversity." Training, Jan. 1992, pp. 23–30.

Jamieson, D., and O'Mara, J. Managing Workforce 2000. San Francisco: Jossey-Bass, 1991.

Kanter, R. "The New Managerial Work." Harvard Business Review, 1989, 67 (6), 85–92.

Peters, T. Thriving on Chaos. Schaumburg, Ill.: Harper Perennial, 1987.

Thomas, R. R., Jr. "From Affirmative Action to Affirming Diversity." Harvard Business Review 68 (2), 1990, pp. 107–117.

Thomas, R. R., Jr. Beyond Race and Gender. New York: American Management Association, 1991.

RUTH BURGOS-SASSCER is president of San Antonio College, San Antonio, Texas. From 1988 until 1993 she was vice president for faculty and instruction at Harry S. Truman College, Chicago.

In a learning organization, elaborate structures, chain of command, and approving and authorizing are unnecessary. Rather, power— meaning the ability to make things happen—is learned within each part of the organization.

Leadership in the Learning Organization

Margaret Gratton

"All life is an experiment. The more experiments you make, the better."

—Ralph Waldo Emerson

Anyone paying attention to the current state of affairs in government, politics, education, business, religion, and even families knows that we are experiencing a leadership crisis. Questions considered simple in the past, such as "Who's in charge?" "Where are we going?" or "May I speak to the head of the household?" now may elicit complex disagreements, even hostility, rather than clear, direct answers. In the mythical good old days, when leadership supposedly flourished, we did not need to struggle in search for leadership. Leaders were easily identifiable. We knew the leaders were those who had titles, held prestigious positions, possessed power and authority. Leaders made the decisions. We could not miss them, for often they carried or wore symbols of their leadership, such as scepters in their hands, stars on their shoulders, mitres on their heads. Leaders presided over things from large, well-appointed offices. They were privy to special information and special privileges. They had other people serve them and give them, promptly, things they wanted or needed. Leaders appeared at the peak of the organizational pyramid or in the top box, front and center, in the classical organizational chart.

In community colleges, leadership meant the chancellor or president and an executive cabinet accountable to a board of trustees. Born out of postwar optimism and into the military-industrial complex, early community colleges

NEW DIRECTIONS FOR COMMUNITY COLLEGES, no. 84, Winter 1993 © Jossey-Bass Publishers

were modeled on strong, top-down leadership and classical-scientific management techniques, tempered by something called collegiality. Three generations later these influences are still prevalent. Yet notions of leadership are undergoing change, and old management techniques have become increasingly frustrating.

The perceived need for good leaders is as strong as ever, yet many are discouraged and even cynical about the state of leadership. In recent Harris polls, public perception of leadership is reported as appallingly low, with 53 percent of the adults in one survey expressing alienation from those in leadership positions. Only 10 percent expressed confidence in business leaders, and a mere 14 percent trusted labor leaders (Oakley and Krug, 1991, p. 175).

During recent interviews for the selection of an academic vice president at a West Coast community college, a candidate asked committee members, "What do you want your new vice president to be or to do?" One replied, "A philosopher-king," another said, "To walk on water," and yet another noted, "To bring vision to our reality." Each of the committee members is an experienced academic manager, serving in an important leadership position. Each knows well the challenge of leadership, yet, in a sense, each asked the impossible of a future leader of their own. Inherent in each comment was a mix of frustration with the status quo, an implicit expression of powerlessness, and a belief that someone, not currently part of the system, could arrive and set it all right, even transform it. How would that happen? What techniques could this remarkable individual bring to bear on the institution not now considered or applied by the present leaders? And why?

In his 1990 study of management techniques in community colleges, Deegan (1992) asked 311 community college CEOs to report which management techniques they were using in the areas of planning, organizing, budgeting, staffing, and evaluation. Further, the CEOs were asked to indicate which of the management practices used they would rate as "very successful" (Deegan, 1992, p. 27). The discrepancy between the number of techniques used and the small number of techniques rated as "very successful" was nothing short of discouraging. After a generation of staff development programs, agendas for excellence, and an explosion of literature on leadership as an art and management as a scientific discipline, community college CEOs still cite insufficient resources and disgruntled, inflexible staff as their greatest problems. Somehow this does not bode well for the future of community colleges or any other organization caught in a struggle with diminishing fiscal resources and allegedly unyielding human spirit.

Leadership: A State of Mind

Whether we admit it or not, many of our notions of leadership are heavily dominated by power and profit motifs. The one who controls and distributes the resources to result in maximum return is given deference as a leader, although the techniques employed may be purely managerial. The controller of resources invariably inherits the power to control and shape the environment, while subordinates, those not in control, comply with this sometimes inadvertent form of leadership. Consequently, in thinking about leadership as power and profit-making, we may often overlook extraordinary feats of human achievement through effective leadership practices in the arts (stage, film, music, dance), education in the classroom, and athletics. In these spheres, individual and ensemble achievements reflect the power of artistic directors, teachers, and coaches to tap into real talent and let it flourish.

Recently I asked a friend what qualities he would want in a leader. This friend is the head of an academic department and has a history of successful coaching and athletic accomplishments. I knew his answer would be based on solid personal experience as a team member and a follower, as well as being a leader. He, indeed, had a ready response, honed from half a lifetime of athletic competition, of surviving, working, and managing in small and large structured systems. "Sincerity," he said, "someone who is genuine and genuinely cares. Someone who has knowledge and expertise, and, finally, there must be integrity. A leader must be someone you can trust." The directness of his answer and its lack of inaccessible or complex notions was both reassuring and disarming. It was reassuring to hear the espousal of traditional and familiar leadership characteristics; it was disarming to think that, given these valued characteristics, why do so many perceive current leadership as ineffective? Could it be that the way we persist in thinking about leadership and the actual requirements of contemporary leadership are no longer congruent?

I asked an actor how a good director is a good leader. The actor spoke of trust and how a skillful director has a coherent concept that can be expressed to others. The director both teaches and coaches the individual actor and the acting ensemble. Finally, the actor recalled a particularly effective director who, when an actor was blocked and when repeated attempts at an apparently logical dramatic technique had failed, would suggest trying an opposite technique. Stepping apart from the predictable and prescribed, the actors found freedom for creative expression, risk taking, and professional learning. Because the director encouraged the actors' creativity and then ensured safety and support in the process, the actors grew and productions were rich with the best results of experimentation. The power of this example is that the director did not dictate, control, or threaten but did assume that the actor had the capability to do something creative and then directed on that basis.

During the 1980s, management and leadership books flourished expounding everything from Tao principles rendered in Pooh Bear language, to the evolution of strategic planning, to the current phenomenon of total quality management or continuous improvement. What did not get properly questioned in this onslaught of organizational "self-help" was the fundamental assumptions on which notions of leadership and management are founded. Before any change can occur, before we can find effective leaders now or for the twenty-first century, we need to examine how we think about organizations and how we think about leaders, people, and work. Our personal management style (MS) will persist in predictably frustrating practices, until we free ourselves to think in ways that are congruent with the nature of people using and working in our organizations.

One of the most strikingly persistent beliefs about leadership is that a leader is one who does something to us or for us. This opinion can result in idealization of the leader and quickly converts to disillusionment, even cynicism, when the leader fails to deliver. The belief that the leader acts on us is rooted in an assumed passivity on the part of followers. It means that the leader is a discrete powerful individual charged with bringing everything and everyone along. Others do as the leader decides and, unless so charged, remain dependent and passive. In spite of an era of empowerment theories and techniques for "empowered managers" (Block, 1989), the persistence of passivity and dependence is rampant. Followers still want to know what leaders will do for them—possible leaders being classroom instructors, deans, presidents, labor leaders, elected officials, heads of state, or the chair of any committee.

By the same token, leaders who believe that they must do everything for others and control all events easily grow discouraged with impossible situations. They may never understand that their overwrought sense of responsibility and need for control is rooted in basic assumptions that their followers are incapable, unprepared, and unable to initiate action without the directives of leadership. They may never understand that their so-called followers behave passively because they are viewed as followers and believe themselves to be lacking opportunity or competence for initiative.

In a sense, our traditional ways of thinking about leadership are almost painfully simplistic. We define leadership by describing qualities the leader ought to possess. By the same token, we typically define management by compiling lists of management techniques to implement. This kind of discrete unit thinking cuts staff off from thinking deeply about the complexity of relationships, dynamics, and interplay that results in human accomplishment. Leadership does not occur in a vacuum. As an abstraction it is merely a mind game. Leadership occurs in time, space, setting, and relationships with other people. It is grounded in thought, action, and interaction. It is born out of fundamental assumptions and beliefs about the purpose of life, the nature of human beings, the significance of ourselves as individuals in relation to others and the world we live in. Leadership literally is a state of being, a state of mind, a way of thinking that translates to behaviors that produce desired results. Leadership discussions focus endlessly on observed behaviors without considering the state of mind, belief systems, and mental models that drive leadership and management behavior.

Controlling and Learning Organizations

Recently I worked with my students in an organizational systems and development class to design an "organization continuum." We built a linear scale of organization models, indicating the style of leadership required. We considered ways in which the organizational structure and leadership style reflected fundamental assumptions about the individual, the worker, the human members of the organizational system.

We began with organization by domination characterized by subordination, conscription, brute force, and use of fear. We labeled it the Egyptian Pyramid model. In such a system, leadership assumes that the individual is not an individual but a mere tool, a means to an end, valued only for physical strength and stamina. We went on to organization by classical management, the Prussian Army model. The individual is again not valued as an individual, but as part of an orderly whole. Leadership's charge is to maintain order through unity and line of command. Harmony and order are achieved by obedience and rigorous discipline. Next was Frederick Taylor's model of scientific management, which emphasizes the individual as an economic unit. Application of scientific principles to selection of workers, design and flow of work, and time and motion studies results in productivity and profit.

The students worked right on through organization by bureaucracy, where the individual is valued as a functionary, and performance is governed by standardized roles and examinations. They advanced to the Country Club model, organization by human relations. Enter the individual at last, valued for his or her own sake. This familiar model assumes the truth of Maslow's hierarchy of needs and democratic principles, and it warmly embraces human potential. The class charged onward to organization by systems, which assumes the individual to be self-regulatory as well as interdependent and interrelated within an open system environment. Finally, they concluded the continuum with the learning organization, which assumes the individual to be capable of transformation, peak performance, and synergistic relationships. Some referred to this as the "harmonic convergence" model.

While the students had fun in working with the continuum, they also saw an evolution in organizational, management, and leadership thinking. But, most importantly, they saw how assumptions about the individual and the nature of work drive leadership models as well as organizational structures. In the challenging pursuit of effective leadership we should ask not "What should I do?" but "What do I think? What should I think and how should I think?" In looking at the organization-management-leadership continuum, the reason we are having difficulty with leadership becomes clear. The continuum reveals how, until very recently, leadership was hierarchical, controlling, authoritarian, centralized, and based on a purely pragmatic view of the individual. In turn, the individual existing within the organization was expected to follow orders, obey rules, and perform productively for profit making or efficiently for the sake of order. The inherent assumption was that people could not manage themselves, might make mistakes if not controlled, and did not have sufficient ability or perspective to think for themselves or for the well-being of the organization. These assumptions continue today.

Most of us have been exposed, in varying degrees, to these leadership characteristics and assumptions. Through socialization in organizations, we carry vestiges of domination, a desire for control and for others to do our bidding. In some cases, it is more than vestiges. Presidents and deans occupy leadership positions who were specifically trained in leadership by rank and who assume that those lower in rank are less competent. Tight control of people, events, and resources is equated with effectiveness.

And, finally, many of us have had our own sense of self-worth challenged through structures of domination including family, school, church, military, the workplace, and organizational systems. The patriarchal cornerstones of Western civilization are based on the need for an appointed hero to redeem the helpless and hapless masses. Cultural assumptions run deep and produce a "power-over" consciousness of control, regulation, and compliance (Starhawk, 1989, p. 14). As powerful and enduring as this consciousness is, it no longer is effective in the late twentieth century. We have watched major political structures and systems of control crumble, from corporations to political regimes. Yet, are we really thinking in new ways about leadership, systems, and organizations? Thinking results in attitudes, behavior, and action. Quite simply, if we want different results we must develop a new kind of mind (Lynch and Kordis, 1988, p. 21) and new ways of seeing things.

Dramatic shifts in thinking about leadership and effective organizations have been evolving for at least twenty years. During this time, nothing can match the impact of the work of W. Edwards Deming and his quality revolution (Gabor, 1990). Whether or not one agrees with Deming's views of quality, process analysis, and customer delight, his thinking is changing how U.S. organizations operate and what leadership means. Unfortunately, Deming's fundamental views, his breakthrough assumptions about how human effort continually improves, often get lost in oversimplified, trendy, hyped versions of how to get better, be better, and make more money fast. Ironically, a body of thought that the Nike Company distilled to "There is no finish line" still elicits responses like, "Total quality management is just fine, but I want something to give me results right now." Once again, those in charge are looking for a laundry list of discrete things to do, which will result in immediate change that will, in turn, produce a sense of control. This is, quite simply, leadership and management at its most shallow level. The new assumptions, the new ways of thinking may get lost in the focus on short-term action rather than thinking about the principles and the relationships that will shape action.

It is a challenge to rethink organizational processes based on systems theory or variation principles. It is a challenge to understand the multiplier effect of unhappy staff and incompetent work or, conversely, well-trained staff and satisfied clients. What does it mean to develop a college's core competencies, to believe in the strength of the "intrinsic motivation" of all people? How do we come face to face with the presence of anxiety in our organizations? Why might we give lip service to eliminating anxiety and still subtly cultivate it as a means of control? Do we still believe in fear as a motivator and, if so, on what assumptions is that based? What is the relationship of fear and impaired performance? How do leaders and managers cease working as discrete units and begin to see themselves as part of an interdependent system, in charge of learning—their own learning and the learning of all who work with them? How do leaders assimilate the principle that if learning is continuous, change and improvement will be continuous also? Nothing will ever be frozen in time or space. The process will always be "in process." The Deming principles ask leaders and managers to stop counting and begin thinking. Begin thinking about the processes, the relationships, the cause and effect systems, the envisioned and desired outcomes of which numerical quality may be only one of many significant variations.

The total quality management and continuous improvement movement is now becoming institutionalized in the United States. Any day of the week one may choose from an array of seminars and workshops that will teach how to do it in a weekend or eight hours or less. The movement is popularized. Articles and literature abound. Some major corporations have done the deep thinking and have patiently and persistently worked through changes in assumptions, actions, and outcomes. Whether the tag TQM survives or not, the popularity of the movement is changing our thinking about leadership and control. In some cases, it may be inadvertent, almost by osmosis. In other cases, change is occurring from continuous thinking and experimentation. And, finally, new voices are emerging to carry the new thought processes to the next level of understanding.

Leadership as Learning and Continuous Improvement

The continuous improvement paradigm is rooted in a total and vigorous organizational commitment to training, education, and self-improvement. At a more conceptual level, it requires that questioning, thinking, and innovating be as essential to the organization as breathing. Practitioners interested in continuous improvement must ask, How is this to be done? A powerful design for creating and nurturing an environment for learning throughout an organization is offered by Peter Senge in *The Fifth Discipline: The Art and Practice of the Learning Organization*. Senge (1990) defines the learning organization as one that is "continually expanding its capacity to create its future" (p. 14). This notion goes beyond simple improvement and brings thinking to a creative level. The underlying leadership assumption is that staff long to learn and need to learn to generate initiative. Adaptive learning allows one to survive.

Generative learning, involving ideas, experimentation, innovation, and initiative, leads to creation of a learning culture in the organization.

Applied to leadership and management, these assumptions move us away from traditional top-down management, from unquestioning adherence to policy, regulations, and structures, from controlling, competing, and counting. Every aspect of Senge's "metanoic" (shift of the mind) organization (p. 13) is rooted in learning, from developing a system's view, to cultivating personal mastery, to questioning and rethinking assumptions, to having a shared vision, to team learning. In such an environment there is no need for a philosopher king, a miracle worker, a messianic personality. There is no need for elaborate structures, chain of command, and approving and authorizing. There is no sense of the word empowerment as something one does to another. Rather, power, meaning the "ability to make things happen," is learned within each part of the organization. Each part of the organization continually learns of the interrelatedness of parts and how the organization can be strengthened. Academic departments learn of their importance to the whole organization and other academic departments. Service units learn about their relationship to academic departments and how together they help the organization achieve its goals.

The assumption that learning is at the heart of continuous improvement and that learning creates the future dramatically changes prevailing beliefs about leadership in community colleges. In a learning organization, effective leadership may emerge anywhere true learning is taking place. Leadership occurs where there is competence and innovation. Leadership is the ability to coach, teach, and interpret reality with others as they learn. Leadership may be continually shifting and changing as learning occurs. It ceases being exclusive, authoritative, or untouchable. Leadership is learned and earned, not assumed. Its power becomes "power-with" (working in partnership with others) and "power-within" (personal competence).

For the jaded among us, who cringe at the thought of one more discussion of leadership or who are scarred from past, unhappy experiments, this may all seem hopelessly idealistic. Nevertheless, major organizations are using these learning principles, such as Royal Dutch Shell, Hanover Insurance, and Kyocera (Senge, 1990, p. 140), Florida Light and Power, Federal Express, Motorola, and Glove Metallurgical (Bowles and Hammond, 1991).

Let us revisit Deegan's survey of community college CEOs and the use of management techniques. Absent from the list of items was any reference to systems thinking or organizational learning. One ray of insight was related to staff development. Of those community college CEOs who had set up full-time offices for professional development, 60 percent found the results to be very successful, but relatively few (12 percent) had made such a move. In light of new and emerging organizational, leadership, and management thinking, Deegan's survey items, based on control through planning, organizing, budgeting, staffing, and evaluation, were woefully inadequate. The responses reflected status quo notions about management and leadership. All of the management techniques were treated as discrete factors. No technique addressed systems thinking or cultivation of organizational learning.

Our community colleges, as centers of learning, cannot fail to be less than learning organizations themselves. The assumptions about product, client delight, continuous improvement—assumptions about learning as central to creation of the future—will change teaching and learning throughout the institution, in and out of the classroom. The American Association of Community Colleges' policy for institutional effectiveness, developed by the National Consortium for Institutional Effectiveness and Student Success, articulates a national vision for community colleges related to systems thinking and organizational learning ("AACC Policy Statement," 1992). This is an important document, but making the move from words on paper to a transformed organization is a long, arduous trip. It will require that elusive quality of leadership for all who take the journey.

We might return to the thoughts of the athlete and the actor, for they expressed similar notions in different ways. The athlete spoke of genuine caring. That is a passionate concern for the human spirit and commitment to cultivating what is good. He spoke of expertise, which is leadership grounded in learning, competence, and continuous improvement. Finally, he talked of integrity, congruency of thought, word, behavior, and action—the foundation of trust. The actor also spoke of trust as fundamental. He described the director teaching, coaching, and being able to express a creative concept for and with the acting ensemble. Is this not shared vision, team learning, and mastery? The actor spoke respectfully of the director who assumed the creative competence of the actor, asked the actor to risk, and then honored and made safe the creative experiment.

All of these characteristics are familiar and continue to endure as desired leadership qualities. But in the community college as a learning organization, these valued qualities cannot be the exclusive realm of a small group of executive managers. These are qualities desired for instructors and staff in order to flourish, literally to grow in abundance. Leadership is a state of mind that assumes learning is essential and that the future is created by living through complexity with competency and vision.

Tomorrow's Leaders in Community Colleges

There is no lack of leaders in community colleges; rather, we seem to be on a singular and narrow road looking for a Wizard of Oz to give us something we already have. Perhaps the current cynicism toward leadership reflects a frustration with ourselves and our own inclinations toward passivity—our misplaced hope that someone else will give us what we think we need.

In tomorrow's community colleges, the individual—that is, each of us— is assumed to be an agent of transformation. Implicit in this assumption is the commitment so valued by the athlete and the actor to learning processes and to creativity. The implications for leadership are not easy. They are, in fact, demanding.

Argyris has written about the dark side of the learning imperative—that organizational inquiry and development can be threatening. Typically, staff are not rewarded for asking tough questions, identifying complex problems, or pointing out dysfunctional processes or relationships. It is not good form to appear uncertain or ignorant. So organizations persist in, as Senge put it, "skilled incompetence" or "organizational disability" (Argyris, 1970, p. 25).

Argyris's theories of learning provide an excellent road map for self-renewing leadership. Fundamental to learning is information freely available and processed. When information is accessible, processed, and applied, decision making is demystified. Issues do not have to be sent off for consideration by power figures far from the locus of action. The sphere of control and influence broadens to include instructors, staff, and students. Those currently in leadership positions have the capability to open up information processes and provide training and development for staff in the use of information for organizational improvement. Through learning based on good information, those currently in leadership positions can let go of the burden of control. They can extend it to others, who also through learning can make informed choices about work processes and how things fit together. A commitment to learning can build collective understanding and a sense of purpose. Learning contributes to self-confidence, competence, and informed communications. Learning can improve trust, keeping in mind that lack of trust invariably is rooted in poor information or poor processing of information.

Senge (1990) speaks of the "quiet design work of leadership." It is, perhaps, an answer for those who wonder where to begin. One begins to rethink leadership first by choosing to change, to rethink old assumptions, to question. What are we doing? Who is doing it? Why are we doing it? How are we doing? How can we do it better? How are we all connected? Then the design of leadership, the design of the system, emerges answer by answer, step by step, choice by choice. Each person learns; each unit learns; the organization learns. Learning is a developmental process, and leadership emerges out of it. This is a major shift from the tradition of leadership, derived from title and office, issuing top-down directives to be followed without question, without thinking. The "quiet design of leadership" assumes that staff desire to learn and thrive on learning, and through learning they can shape their own destiny.

What does this mean for leadership in our community colleges? It means cultivating a system's view of our colleges and understanding the inner-connectedness of all processes; designing a free flow of information, readily available and understandable for informed decision making and perspective; committing to learning as a "constant" in the system and ensuring full support for continual learning and development; understanding that learning is developmental and requires design, planning, time, support, patience, and persistence. It means acting on the fact that vision, planning, total quality management, and institutional effectiveness cannot work by leadership edict, by just being written down or talked about. Each must be learned and lived. It means embracing organizational learning so leadership will be a responsibility shared by all members based on understanding, competence, and creativity. Leaders must accept the risks of candor, shared responsibility, and trust, honoring each person's intrinsic power to learn to contribute and create the future.

How does this happen in community colleges?

Still we might ask, Who begins the task of redesigning leadership in the learning organization? What is the first step? Nothing happens unless someone inside or outside the organization acts to make it happen. The challenge to start the work of a new leadership imperative lies with current leaders— those who presently serve as our college presidents, deans, department chairs. As leaders they are expected to know what to do next. They must ask the right questions, rethink old assumptions, and begin the experiments of change. They must start the learning process that will weave its way through the entire organization, connecting individuals, processes, outcomes. If done with passion and persistence, our community colleges will become learning organizations based on genuine caring, competence, and continuous improvement.

Finally, our colleges will be true organizational models of the spirit of learning—the very purpose for which they exist.

References

"AACC Policy Statement on Institutional Effectiveness." Washington, D.C.: American Association of Community Colleges, 1992.

Argyris, C. Intervention Theory and Method. Reading, Mass.: Addison-Wesley, 1970.

Block, P. The Empowered Manager. San Francisco: Jossey-Bass, 1987.

Bowles, J., and Hammond, J. Beyond Quality. New York: Berkeley Books, 1991.

Deegan, W. L. "Proven Techniques: The Use and Impact of Major Management Concepts in Community Colleges." Community Technical and Junior College Journal, 1992, 62 (5), 26–30.

Gabor, A. The Man Who Discovered Quality. New York: Penguin Books, 1990.

Lynch, D., and Kordis, P. Strategy of the Dolphin: Scoring a Win in a Chaotic World. New York: Fawcett Columbine, 1988.

Oakley, E., and Krug, D. Enlightened Leadership: Why Pay Someone Else to Tell Your People What They Already Know. Denver: Stonetree, 1992.

Senge, P. The Fifth Discipline: The Art and Practice of the Learning Organization. New York: Doubleday, 1990.

Starhawk. Truth or Dare. San Francisco: HarperCollins, 1989.

MARGARET GRATTON is assistant to the president for staff and organization development at Mt. Hood Community College, Gresham, Oregon. She also serves at Portland State University as an adjunct faculty member in organizational systems.

An annotated bibliography is provided on various aspects of the changing face of management within the community college, including information on adapting to change, changing roles with administrative structures, and the appearance of new players in administrative activities.

Sources and Information: The Dynamics of Change in Managerial Responsibilities and Roles

David Deckelbaum

Managing and providing leadership in today's community colleges require a leader to personally embrace change and promote an acceptance of change in others. The successful administration of a community college may involve new models of governance, enlarged roles for some players, the inclusion of stakeholders previously unrepresented or underrepresented, and a host of problems caused by shifting demographics, changing educational and societal needs, and an era of financial instability.

This chapter presents citations that reflect the current ERIC literature on issues that surround the management and administration of community colleges. Most ERIC documents (references with "ED" numbers) can be viewed on microfiche at approximately 900 libraries worldwide. In addition, most documents may be ordered on microfiche or in paper copy from the ERIC Document Reproduction Service (EDRS) at (800) 443-ERIC.

Adapting to Change

These materials demonstrate the need to view change from many perspectives and to understand that the change process involves the entire institution and all of its constituents.

Baker, G. A. III, and others. *Cultural Leadership: Inside America's Community Colleges.* Washington, D.C.: American Association of Community and Junior Colleges, 1992. 71 pp. (ED 350 049). Available from the American Association of Community and Junior Colleges (AACJC), Publications Sales, P.O. Box 1737, Salisbury, MD 21802 ($27.50; $23 for AACJC members).

Contending that the relationship between leadership and the creation and management of institutional culture is critical to the future success of community colleges, this volume explores theory, research, and practice associated with this perspective. The following chapters are provided: (1) "Creative Cultures: Toward a New Paradigm" by George A. Baker III, (2) "Community College Climate: The Signature of a Movement" by George A. Baker III, (3) "Creating, Managing, and Transforming Community College Culture: Presidential Perspectives" by Charlotte Biggerstaff, (4) "Culture and Communication" by Tessa Martinez Tagle, (5) "Empowering the Leadership Team" by Mary Ann Roe, (6) "Instructional Leadership: Building a Culture of Excellence in the Teaching-Learning Community" by Rosemary Gillett-Karam and Eli Pena, (7) "An Organizational Culture Consciously Shaped to Foster Creativity and Innovation" by Michele Nelson, (8) "Cultural Leadership: The Founder" by Phyllis Barber, (9) "Cultural Leadership: The Successor" by Phyllis Barber, (10) "Culture, Leadership, and Organizational Systems" by G. Allan Clark, and (11) "The Future of the Community College in Evolution: Approaches to Analysis of Organizational Culture and Functioning" by George A. Baker III. A 286-item bibliography is included.

Dance, T. "Leadership & Spirit: Rejuvenating an Organization from the Bottom Up." Paper presented at the annual conference of the Association of Canadian Community Colleges, Winnipeg, Manitoba, Canada, May 1991. 43 pp. (ED 332 736)

Using a case study that documents the creation of the Access and Program Development Division at George Brown College, a large urban community college in Ontario, Canada, this paper explores the nature of leadership in educational management. Introductory material argues that leadership in management should be defined as a performing art rather than a science. Next, a four-page literature review examines the trend away from a structured, goal-directed approach to management toward a more spiritual, self-reflective one and contrasts works on traditional and nontraditional approaches to leadership. The case study is then presented in the following sections: (1) The Parable of the Seeds, or the Story of the Access Division; (2) Access Division—History and Achievements, reporting quantifiable indicators of success, academic upgrading, services for the hearing impaired and special needs students, and community outreach; (3) tables examining the Access Division's structure and achievements from 1989 to 1991; (4) an analysis of the case study, using a framework that focuses on structure, people, politics, and symbols/spirit; and (5) a conclusion, underscoring the importance of the leader's ability to view the organization through multiple lenses. Attachments include "One Leader's Creed for the Workplace," twenty references, and an information flyer on the Access Division.

Gilley, J. W. Thinking About American Higher Education: The 1990s and Beyond. New York: Macmillan, 1991. 214 pp. (ED 331 401). Available from Macmillan Publishing Company, 866 Third Ave., New York, NY 10022 ($27.95).

This book explores three major imperatives of American higher education in the decades ahead. First, colleges and universities will be required to respond to six critical challenges: minority participation, financing quality education, replacing quality faculty, affordability, institutional ethics, and national competitiveness. Second, strong leadership will be required at both the institutional and state government levels. Third, the impact of changing regional economies will transform institutions located in burgeoning metropolitan areas and foster new forms of higher education. Seventeen chapters address these and other issues, including the community college perspective (in a chapter by George B. Vaughan), leadership of governors versus college presidents, U.S. higher education as a managerial model, multicampus governing boards, coordinating boards and the politicization of U.S. higher education, new ways of serving hypergrowth regions (in a chapter by Edward L. Delaney and Donald M. Norris), and the distributed university. An appendix reports on a 1988–89 survey of 148 college and university presidents, governors, and others that identified respondents' opinions on important issues, trends, challenges, and troubling patterns. References are provided for each chapter.

Messina, R. C., and Fagans, A. C. "Assessment: What's the Next Step? A Model for Institutional Improvement." Paper presented at the Annual Summer Institute on Community College Effectiveness and Student Success, Vail, Colo., June 21–24, 1992. 14 pp. (ED 348 118)

Institutional change requires that "restraining" forces (those forces resisting change) be minimized and "driving" forces (those forces moving in the direction of change) be maximized. Lasting change involves broad-based staff participation in the change process; this requires the establishment of multiple feedback levels or linkages. The institutional change model adapted by Burlington County College (BCC) in Pemberton, New Jersey, is based on extensive feedback providing "informational linkages" necessary for change. The model has three components: (1) the "improvement area," consisting of the issues and structures in need of change identified through outcomes assessment procedures; (2) "institutional culture," including those aspects of leadership, governance, climate, faculty professionalism, external regulations, funding, enrollment, community, and the assessment structure that affect the specific improvement areas identified; and (3) "results of the change process," including changes in goals, objectives, and assessment methods that have resulted from the implementation of new procedures, policies, and curriculum. In an effort to minimize the restraining forces and maximize the driving forces affecting efforts to bring about change within the Basic Skills Program (BSP) at BCC, several activities were undertaken. Data on state-mandated assessment were presented at the first semester faculty meeting. Task forces were convened to analyze the BSP, and informal discussion groups were held. A basic skills handbook was created, a review of the reading program was scheduled, and special support was provided for faculty involved in computer/video instruction.

Changing Roles

Institutional restructuring and new models of governance provide an environment that fosters a continual reevaluation of leadership roles within administrative structures.

Parsons, M. H. Enhancing Teaching–Learning Environments: A Change Management Strategy. Hagerstown, Md.: Hagerstown Junior College, 1991. 9 pp. (ED 333 926)

The 1990s may well be characterized as the decade of renewal. For community colleges, the process of renewal will entail refocusing the mission and redefining the culture of two-year institutions as part of a nationwide attempt to restructure our approach to higher education. But is it possible to modify both college mission and culture? Since change has become the hallmark of contemporary society, we have the unenviable task of managing the process or being overwhelmed by it. Managing change in this period of restructuring should begin with an examination of organizational values. Values clarification, in turn, starts with a review of institutional purpose. An assessment of purpose allows all groups within an institution to develop insights regarding organizational beliefs; orientation toward clients; treatment of human, fiscal, and physical assets; and salience of mission. The assessment process, which should include a review of college practices that affect the teaching–learning environment, supports the institutional community in redesigning and reordering the processes, procedures, and systems that comprise culture. Once the redefinition of organizational purpose is established, culture will reform itself around the redefined purpose. The new system evolves by establishing a shared vision of the future. Researchers suggest that if institutional values are clear, shared, and affirmed in action, personnel are likely to trust the organization and work to implement its stated purposes.

The Top Ten Issues Facing America's Community Colleges. 1991 Edition. Warren, Mich.: Macomb Community College, Institute for Future Studies, 1991. 28 pp. (ED 327 248)

This paper, designed to identify and describe the key challenges facing community colleges as a result of major changes in the social, economic, and demographic makeup of students and service areas, combines information gathered from two national environmental scanning groups, a review of the literature, and input from educational professionals. The ten community college issues discussed are as follows: (1) increasingly diverse service areas and student populations; (2) growing numbers of academically underprepared students; (3) an unclear workforce agenda for the information age; (4) the need to ensure and provide evidence of institutional effectiveness; (5) the need to improve college governance by developing boards of trustees that have vision and purpose and are goal-driven, unified, supported by inspired leadership, and politically astute; (6) the need to promote organizational wellness through environmental scanning, broadened redefinition of college purpose, emphasis on quality, and concern for employee and public opinions; (7) an impending faculty shortage and the aging of the existing faculty; (8) the need for a resurgence of campus collegiality; (9) the impact of external forces, including business people, lay citizens, and legislators, on college governance and decision making; and (10) the role of ethics in institutional management and curriculum. Each topic section concludes with a series of specific questions to initiate further discussion.

Vaughan, G. B. Leadership in Transition: The Community College Presidency. Washington, D.C.: American Association of Community and Junior Colleges, and American Council on Education, 1989. 146 pp. (ED 311 960). Available from American Council on Education/Macmillan Publishing Company, Front and Brown Streets, Riverside, NJ 08075 ($29.95).

Stemming from the author's personal experiences, interviews, research, and needs expressed by individuals in the community college field, this book examines issues currently facing community college presidents and argues for a change in leadership to meet the needs of a new era in higher education. Chapter one briefly describes the role of the founding presidents of community colleges in fostering growth during the 1960s and early 1970s, arguing that the current community college presidency lacks a comparable focus. After chapter two discusses the role of the president as educational leader, chapter three suggests that presidents place a greater distance between themselves and their various constituencies by delegating authority and extricating themselves from mundane campus activities. Chapter four addresses the question of the appropriate length of tenure for a college president, providing a tentative list of signs that indicate a president has been in office too long. Chapters five and six draw from survey data to consider the special problems and advantages faced by women, African-American, and Hispanic presidents. Using information from a national survey of current deans of instruction, chapter seven compares the characteristics of current and past presidents with those who will be presidents in the future. Finally, chapter eight offers practical advice for those who make the community college presidency their career goal, including a list of suggestions for seeking the office.

Wirth, P. L. Shared Governance: Promises and Perils. Marysville, Calif.: Yuba Community College District, 1991. 10 pp. (ED 331 568)

Shared governance in the community college district has both advantages and disadvantages. The three "perils" of implementing shared governance are that the process is difficult, lengthy, and sometimes tedious; that responsibility for decisions and actions must somehow be maintained; and that an appropriate role for faculty, staff, and administrators must be established and recognized by all participating individuals. Reaching a consensus in decision-making requires that all parties be adequately informed of the issues. However, disseminating such information is not always conducive to effective management. In addition, teaching and learning may become secondary priorities as representatives are away from work or the classroom. Finally, special interest groups may try to misuse the power of shared governance to forward their own agendas, rather than working for the good of the district. While clear perils exist, shared governance promises many rewards, including the empowerment of participants, development of collegial relationships for an improved college environment, greater understanding among employees at all levels about the issues facing their community colleges, and improved communication. The participants in shared governance decisions are more likely to support policies that they have had a role in forming and are more likely to take personal responsibility for the outcomes of such decisions. As representatives in the group decision-making process report back to constituents, collegewide communication and understanding is greatly enhanced, improving the overall college environment.

New Players

Faculty, staff, and students are now participating in the governance of many institutions. This involvement includes membership on committees and task forces dealing with all aspects of community college life.

Franklin, H. D., Burgos-Sasscer, R., Kessel, B., and Mack, J. "Faculty Leadership: A Dynamic, Potent Force for Comprehensive Institutional Development." Paper presented at Leadership 2000, the annual conference on leadership development of the League for Innovation in the Community College, Chicago, Ill., July 7–10, 1991. 14 pp. (ED 344 629)

Responding to the crisis in leadership at community colleges, scholars and practitioners alike have called for a new style of leadership capable of adapting and responding easily to an uncertain political and social climate. Although community colleges are rooted historically in a hierarchical leadership mode, there seems to be broad consensus today that collective leadership is more effective. In specific cases, faculty at community colleges have identified hierarchical leadership structures at their institutions as ineffectual and in need of change. However, despite the fact that community college faculty are uniquely qualified for and desire leadership roles in a collective model, divisions between the faculty and the administration restrict their leadership potential.

Initiating a participatory leadership model requires new approaches and involves various steps, including the following: (1) building trust in a collective model, and between the various constituencies represented in such a model; (2) developing methods for information sharing between faculty, administrators, and boards of trustees; (3) forging dynamic interactions between the two coexisting lines of administration and decision-making (that is, management and academic), enabling primary members of each group to cross-participate; (4) preserving faculty development in the face of budget problems by providing resources to enhance professional growth in specific disciplines, general education, and management; (5) utilizing technology to "create" time for faculty and administrators to engage in collective leadership efforts; and (6) instituting concrete systems of recognition and reward for faculty involvement. This paper includes seventeen references.

Nussbaum, T. J., Cordero, W. J., and Hake, J. L. Encouraging Greater Student Participation in Governance. Sacramento, Calif.: California Community Colleges, Office of the Chancellor, 1990. 21 pp. (ED 322 955)

In response to legislative mandate, three proposals were developed for encouraging student participation in the governance of California's community colleges and establishing a minimum standard regulation for local procedures. The proposals intend to improve accountability, access to governance mechanisms, the quality and effectiveness of representation, and communication and coordination. They are designed to build a community truly interested in high-quality education; establish a continuity in the relationships between students and college faculty, staff, and administrators; assemble student bodies as a collective whole; and ensure leadership and administrative support. One of the proposals contains a set of actions to be taken by the Board of Governors and Office of the Chancellor. A second proposal contains a parallel set of recommended actions to be taken at the local district level, for example ensuring student membership on statewide and district governance committees and task forces and granting student representatives the same rights and privileges as other members; scheduling meetings to accommodate students' time and resources as much as possible; recognizing the Council of Student Body Governments and local student body governments as the official representatives of the state's community college students; and requiring student representatives to maintain their colleges' scholastic standards. This proposal also recommends that at the state level pertinent documents and materials be made available to students in a timely manner, an orientation and ongoing consultation services be offered to student representatives, a student development office be created, and services be established and maintained to recruit and train students for participation in governance. The final proposal is for a new regulation that would require each district governing board to adopt policies and procedures to provide students with the opportunity to participate effectively in college and district governance.

Stetson, N. E. Collegial Governance at College of Marin: A Governmental Model. Management Report 1989–90/2. Association of California Community College Administrators, 1990. 11 pp. (ED 318 494)

The College of Marin has adopted a model of collegial governance that involves the entire campus community in recommending policies and procedures that determine the rules by which employees and students live. The model, which was designed by a task force representing faculty, staff, and students, is based on the U.S. government model of executive, legislative, and judicial branches. Its major components are an Academic Senate, a Classified Senate, a Student Senate, and a Senate Executive Board. Each of the three senates has two major roles: (1) to review and recommend district policies and college procedures, and (2) to recommend appointments from its membership to college governance committees. The Senate Executive Board is composed of an equal number of representatives from each of the three senates. Proposals for new or changed policies or procedures travel through a number of committees before reaching the Senate Executive Board (comparable to a legislative conference committee), where the proposals are refined using suggestions from the three individual senates. The Board of Trustees has the final authority to veto or amend policies recommended to it by the superintendent/president, who serves as the chair of the Senate Executive Board. The superintendent/president has the authority to change recommended procedures if she or he feels they are not in the college's best interests. Through the collegial governance system, the College of Marin has established committees; these include the Affirmative Action Committee, Employee Development Committee, Planning Committee, and Instructional Equipment Committee. Since the model's implementation, forty-two policies and procedures have been recommended and approved.

DAVID DECKELBAUM is user services coordinator at the ERIC Clearinghouse for Community Colleges, University of California, Los Angeles.

INDEX

Ordering Information

New Directions for Community Colleges is a series of paperback books that provides expert assistance to help community colleges meet the challenges of their distinctive and expanding educational mission. Books in the series are published quarterly in Spring, Summer, Fall, and Winter and are available for purchase by subscription and individually.

Subscriptions for 1993 cost $49.00 for individuals (a savings of 25 percent over single-copy prices) and $72.00 for institutions, agencies, and libraries. Please do not send institutional checks for personal subscriptions. Standing orders are accepted.

Single copies cost $16.95 when payment accompanies order. (California, New Jersey, New York, and Washington, D.C., residents please include appropriate sales tax.) Billed orders will be charged postage and handling.

Discounts for quantity orders are available. Please write to the address below for information.

All orders must include either the name of an individual or an official purchase order number. Please submit your order as follows:
 Subscriptions: specify series and year subscription is to begin
 Single copies: include individual title code (such as CC82)

Mail all orders to:
 Jossey-Bass Publishers
 350 Sansome Street
 San Francisco, California 94104-1342

For single-copy sales outside of the United States, contact:
 Maxwell Macmillan International Publishing Group
 866 Third Avenue
 New York, New York 10022-6221

For subscription sales outside of the United States, contact
 any international subscription agency or Jossey-Bass directly.

OTHER TITLES AVAILABLE IN THE
NEW DIRECTIONS FOR COMMUNITY COLLEGES SERIES
Arthur M. Cohen, Editor-in-Chief
Florence B. Brawer, Associate Editor

**Statement of Ownership,
Management and
Circulation**
(Required by 39 U.S.C. 3685)

(ISSN)

1A. Title of Publication	1B. PUBLICATION NO.	2. Date of Filing
NEW DIRECTIONS FOR COMMUNITY COLLEGES	0 1 9 4 3 0 8	12/13/93

3. Frequency of Issue	3A. No. of Issues Published Annually	3B. Annual Subscription Price
Quarterly	Four (4)	$49.00(personal) $72.00(institutional

4. Complete Mailing Address of Known Office of Publication *(Street, City, County, State and ZIP+4 Code) (Not printers)*

350 Sansome Street, San Francisco, CA 94104-1342 (San Francisco County)

5. Complete Mailing Address of the Headquarters of General Business Offices of the Publisher *(Not printer)*

(above address)

6. Full Names and Complete Mailing Address of Publisher, Editor, and Managing Editor *(This item MUST NOT be blank)*
Publisher *(Name and Complete Mailing Address)*

Jossey-Bass Inc., Publishers (above address)

Editor *(Name and Complete Mailing Address)*

Arthur M. Cohen, ERIC Clearinghouse for Junior Colleges, UCLA, 10880 Wilshire Blvd, Rm 1522, Los Angeles, CA 90024-4116

Managing Editor *(Name and Complete Mailing Address)*

Lynn D. Luckow, President, Jossey-Bass Inc., Publishers (address above)

7. Owner *(If owned by a corporation, its name and address must be stated and also immediately thereafter the names and addresses of stockholders owning or holding 1 percent or more of total amount of stock. If not owned by a corporation, the names and addresses of the individual owners must be given. If owned by a partnership or other unincorporated firm, its name and address, as well as that of each individual must be given. If the publication is published by a nonprofit organization, its name and address must be stated.) (Item must be completed.)*

Full Name	Complete Mailing Address
Macmillan, Inc.	55 Railroad Avenue Greenwich, CT 06830-6378

8. Known Bondholders, Mortgagees, and Other Security Holders Owning or Holding 1 Percent or More of Total Amount of Bonds, Mortgages or Other Securities *(If there are none, so state)*

Full Name	Complete Mailing Address
same as above	same as above

9. For Completion by Nonprofit Organizations Authorized To Mail at Special Rates *(DMM Section 424.12 only)*
The purpose, function, and nonprofit status of this organization and the exempt status for Federal income tax purposes *(Check one)*

(1) ☐ Has Not Changed During Preceding 12 Months   (2) ☐ Has Changed During Preceding 12 Months   *(If changed, publisher must submit explanation of change with this statement.)*

10. Extent and Nature of Circulation *(See instructions on reverse side)*	Average No. Copies Each Issue During Preceding 12 Months	Actual No. Copies of Single Issue Published Nearest to Filing Date
A. Total No. Copies *(Net Press Run)*	1,578	1,581
B. Paid and/or Requested Circulation 1. Sales through dealers and carriers, street vendors and counter sales	190	90
2. Mail Subscription *(Paid and/or requested)*	884	922
C. Total Paid and/or Requested Circulation *(Sum of 10B1 and 10B2)*	1,074	1,012
D. Free Distribution by Mail, Carrier or Other Means Samples, Complimentary, and Other Free Copies	141	141
E. Total Distribution *(Sum of C and D)*	1,215	1,153
F. Copies Not Distributed 1. Office use, left over, unaccounted, spoiled after printing	363	428
2. Return from News Agents	0	0
G. TOTAL *(Sum of E, F1 and 2—should equal net press run shown in A)*	1,578	1,581

11.
I certify that the statements made by me above are correct and complete

Signature and Title of Editor, Publisher, Business Manager, or Owner

Larry Ishii Larry Ishii
Vice President

PS Form 3526, January 1991   *(See instructions on reverse)*